SUMMARY

Summary
  Developing a High-Performance Organization
  Organizations no longer just compete with local rivals. Better and faster communications and transportation mean that distant concerns can easily become local rivals. Also, new competitors are coming onstream all the time. In order to compete in this fast changing environment, your organization needs to become high performing.
  You should examine your organization, identifying where it excels and where there's room for improvement, and implement changes where necessary. Encourage those who work with you to excel at what they do, giving their best to making yours a high-performance organization.
  There are five cornerstones of a high-performing organization. Any examination of your organization for high performance should take each of these into account. First there's the mission statement, embodying your organization's strategy. Second is performance measurement – how you examine internal progress. Third, there's customer orientation, how you're positioned to deal with customers. Fourth is leadership, how you lead for high performance. And finally, there's organizational culture, the way your organization is geared toward high performance.
  Using each cornerstone as a guide, you can ensure your organization is poised for high performance in its internal configuration and how it deals with external factors. You should select the right strategy and focus on your customers. Quality leadership is also important, as are the right human resources policies and management practices. Overall, your organizational culture needs to be geared toward success. These should lead to greater value creation for your organization going forward.
  This book will help you gauge your organization's potential for high performance in terms of its mission statement, performance measurement strategies, customer orientation, leadership, and culture. It will also point to

how each of these can be fully harnessed to make yours a high-performing organization with a competitive edge.

Cross-Functional Strategic Management

Have you ever found that people from different functional units in an organization seem to misunderstand each other? It can be challenging to align functional units, but cross-functional collaboration has never been more important than in contemporary business operations. It's vital that organizations adopt a cross-functional strategy if they are to prosper.

In this book you'll learn about the characteristics of cross-functional management, such as providing leadership to generate synergy.

You'll also learn about the benefits of cross-functional management.

And you'll find out about what actions you'll need to take to support strategic cross-functionality – for example developing a cross-functional culture by encouraging people to share their expertise with others.

This book will also show how knowledge management can help you to further your cross-functional strategies.

Finally, this book will outline the principal knowledge management techniques. These will facilitate the free flow of experience, knowledge, and skills in your organization.

Managing for Rapid Change and Uncertainty

All organizations are confronted by change, regardless of how big they are, how established they are, or what industry they're in. The business environment is forever changing, so organizations must be aware of this and be able to adapt when necessary. Those that adapt well to change will thrive. Those that don't will struggle.

Although there are many benefits to an effective, well prepared, and well managed change process, change can also bring about uncertainty, resistance, and anxiety. It's because of this that change requires strong leadership. And strong leadership requires preparation.

Before implementing change, a manager must prepare to lead the change process, and then prepare the organization for the change. This book will take you through the steps and considerations involved. This preparation is key to guiding your organization though the uncertainty of change.

It will also introduce you to the techniques for implementing change – things like getting people involved and committed to what you're trying to do. You'll also learn about the techniques for sustaining change beyond the period of implementation. This ensures that the new way of doing things becomes an ingrained and central part of the organization's new culture.

Managing High Performers

Your company probably employs a number of high performers. These are the people whose drive, energy, and creativity increase productivity and add value to your organization. As a manager, your high performers are your greatest asset. So you should make every effort to develop their potential and retain them in your organization.

This book describes the common characteristics of high performers, which should help you identify them more easily. It also explains the benefits of retaining them in your organization. You'll discover what motivates and drives high performers. And you'll learn how to develop their potential and keep them inspired and happy.

This book outlines techniques for motivating and developing your high performers. You'll discover how to reward them fairly.

You'll also discover the importance of providing them with meaningful and challenging work. And you'll find out why it's important to allow them to have input into how their work gets done.

Additionally, you'll learn to assign them roles that emphasize their strengths. And finally, you'll learn how you can use mentoring to keep them motivated.

This book also explains how to provide motivating feedback to high performers, which can help you retain them in your organization. And you'll get a chance to practice providing feedback in a simulated scenario.

After taking this book, you'll be better able to develop strategies to help you retain and support the high performers in your organization. In this way, you're more likely to keep your top performers motivated. And you'll be better positioned to tap the great potential they offer your business.

Managing New Managers

A new manager can bring a refreshing approach and perspective that energizes a company.

For instance, a new manager has been hired by a leading manufacturer of medical devices. The new manager is highly educated and has several years of experience with a similar company. The other senior managers of the company hope that this new manager will be able to develop the leadership potential of the company into the future.

To help the new manager reach her full potential, the company has put in place a training program that's designed to help her be successful in her new position. The training program includes providing new manager orientation as well as appointing a senior manager as her mentor.

It's not enough for companies to simply hire new managers and expect them to perform. Companies should invest time and resources in providing training for new managers. This approach will greatly increase the potential of unleashing real leadership abilities in new managers. This book explains and demonstrates training and mentoring techniques that you can use to develop new managers.

Managing Experienced Managers

Experienced managers are potentially a great resource for any organization. They'll have amassed skills and knowledge over a considerable period. But managing such people can present challenges. It sometimes happens that experienced managers neglect their own development, get into the habit of not delegating, or become bored or uninterested. Your role as a manager of experienced managers is to deal with these challenges by steering managers in the right direction.

Organizations must invest in management talent. Attracting and retaining talented managers is important to the leadership potential and growth of the organization. Organizations that fail to retain their top talent risk losing out to competitors.

To retain talented managers, begin by recognizing their potential. Ask yourself who has potential as a leader in the organization. Then you must nurture managers by developing and valuing their knowledge and skills. Use effective coaching to optimize their performance.

This book will help you develop the potential of the experienced managers on your team. You'll find out about techniques for investing in management talent. Then you'll examine the four stages in the coaching process and have an opportunity to practice conducting a coaching session. Next you'll review five valuable techniques for assessing a manager's performance. Finally, you'll be introduced to guidelines for managing a nonperforming manager.

CHAPTER ONE
Developing a High-Performance Organization

Developing a High-Performance Organization

It's important for an organization to strive to be high performing. There are five key internal aspects that should be coordinated in order to achieve this. They are strategy and mission, structures and processes, customer orientation, leadership, and organizational culture. These aspects must be balanced with the numerous external elements, beyond your control, that may nevertheless affect the organization. These include faster and more disruptive change, global competition, political and regulatory changes, and technology.

Mission statements are important strategically in high-performing organizations. The mission statement of a high-performing organization should be well-defined, with its objectives quantifiable, appropriate, and specific. It should also provide a focus to clarify employees' positions within the organization.

In order to become high-performing, an organization's strategic plan should include performance measurements. These measurements must be well-defined, and they must measure the right things. The organization should also delineate benchmarks, timelines, and consequences for failure to achieve measurables.

There are three means by which an organization can become more customer focused. First, the organization needs to have clear approaches to customer recruitment, satisfaction, and commitment. Second, it should align its strategy to achieve value for customers. And finally, it should ensure your employees understand customer needs and expectations, and know how their work contributes to customer service.

There are three primary practices that are characteristic of high-performing leadership. First is achieving a balance between showing concern for people with showing concern for task issues. Second is coaching and managing clear expectations for employees. And third is focusing on larger objectives, not the minutiae of daily business.

An organization's culture includes the shared values, norms, and beliefs of its employees. Some cultures hinder their organizations by being resistant to change. There are five primary characteristics of a high-performance culture. First, the culture fosters a mentality where individuals want to excel – staff members commit to doing their best to help the organization. Second, it's built around clearly-defined strategic goals, so the culture is geared toward fulfilling the organization's strategy.

Third, it reflects and accommodates external factors. A company's culture must adapt to customer needs and other external variables that matter. Fourth, employees have some autonomy – they're given enough freedom to perform at their best. And fifth, open communication prevails – there is genuine and regular dialog between managers and employees.

Factors that bring success

As a manager, you want your organization to work the best it can. Those you manage also want to work in an environment where they can excel. With increasing global competition, it has become essential that organizations become high performing. But what makes an organization perform well?

There are several hallmarks of a high-performing organization. In such organizations everyone works together toward a common goal. The organization has good leadership and stays true to its mission. However, it can and will change when necessary. High-performing organizations also have a culture that encourages communication and continuous learning among those involved.

A high-performing organization is constructed in a way that encourages people to excel. This helps the organization to deliver results time and again. In contrast, a low-performing organization is one where those involved act at cross purposes. Without good leadership and communication, the hard work of those involved is wasted as each person's labor may counteract others' efforts. Organizations are like sports teams. Without adequate coaching, a team's talent is wasted on the playing field.

It's important to strive to become a high-performing organization, as organizations marked by low performance can suffer in many ways. Low performance can lead to employee inefficiency, customer dissatisfaction, and low revenues.

In non-profit organizations, poor performance may drive away those willing to invest time or donate to the organizations' work. This can undermine the organizations' abilities to achieve their goals by jeopardizing much needed resources.

Businesses and other types of organizations are complex systems and there's no one method by which they become high-performing. Achieving the desired level of performance involves coordinating five key internal aspects of your organization. These aspects are strategy and mission, structures and processes, customer orientation, leadership, and finally, organizational culture.

Strategy and mission

Your organization should be built around the vision embodied in its core strategy and mission. These must be aligned with external factors such as the market realities and customer priorities. For example, a mission statement stressing quality and versatility may help a clothing company maintain focus in an ever-changing fashion market.

Structures and processes

Human resources and management processes such as performance measurement should be aligned with strategy. How you organize your employees and measure their performance will impact on how well your strategy is pursued. For instance, regular performance measurement may improve productivity within a manufacturing company.

Customer orientation

Your customers' priorities must drive your business and its strategy. How your organization gauges customers and their needs is of crucial importance. If, for example, your customers require constant technical support, your organization's strategy should be geared toward providing it.

Leadership

What managers do when leading is more important than what they are. Managers contribute significantly to the creation of an organization's culture and the fostering of human resources while also dealing with technical issues. Good managers, for example, realize their employees are the single most important asset they have for success.

Organizational culture

The organizational culture has a bearing on how information is used and what strategic options the organization may consider. A good culture contributes to a company's competitive advantage by aligning with its strategy and core competencies. For example, a technology start-up's culture may prioritize constant innovation and brainstorming.

An organization's customer orientation directly informs its strategy and mission. This strategy and mission feed directly into the organizational culture. The culture is fostered with good leadership. These in turn contribute to the development of structures and processes.

The proper coordination of these internal factors can lead to a work environment where high performance is facilitated and where a strong leadership directs a dynamic organization, populated by satisfied and productive employees.

When developing the internal aspects of your organization, you also need to consider some external elements. These external elements include the available talent, global competition, faster and more disruptive change, and technology. Political and regulatory changes, the influence of ethics, and environmental factors also play a role.

Each of these external factors varies over time and can change how your organization operates in the future. So you need to carefully observe how these factors evolve with relation to your organization.

For instance, over time, customer expectations alter, competitors rise and fall, new technologies come onstream, and various other changes may occur that you'll have to consider. Business success always rests on balancing those external elements outside your control with the internal aspects of your organization that you do have control over.

Importance of mission statements

Mission statements are integral to high-performing organizations. Nearly all leading corporations have a written mission statement. They're short statements that set out an organization's mission and strategic direction, and they communicate the company's purpose to employees and customers alike.

A good mission statement clearly and concisely imparts a company's reason to exist, its goals, and how it will achieve them. This can guide employees and inspire them to contribute to the organization's high performance.

Mission statements must be followed consistently within an organization to be effective. For instance, managers may say that a company's mission statement must be adhered to but fail to stick to it themselves. This can demoralize staff members. They may stop believing anything the managers say. They may also decide that they're allowed to behave in similar ways to the managers, cherry-picking which rules to follow, or ignoring the rules completely. All these things may lead the company to low performance.

In a high-performing organization, the clearly-stated mission statement benefits every part of the organization. Higher up, managers make sure to adhere consistently to the organization's strategic approach. The mission statement helps to align the actions of managers with those of employees.

Employees understand why the organization exists and what direction it's going in. They also see what they're required to do to help the organization develop. Ideally, they may commit to the organization rather than simply comply with its edicts.

You may have suggested several characteristics. However, there are two primary characteristics of a good mission statement. The statement should be well-defined, and it should provide a focal point for employees' actions.

There are three ways in which an organization's mission statement should be well-defined. A well-defined mission statement includes objectives that are quantifiable, appropriate, and specific.

Quantifiable

Your mission statement should have at least one indicator that measures whether the organization's objectives are being achieved. Quantifiable objectives enable an organization to measure whether it's achieving its mission.

Appropriate

The objectives stated in your mission statement should align with the mission and vision of your organization. Setting out a mission and then deviating from it in your mission statement makes the statement less useful to your organization.

Specific

Your mission statement should indicate clearly what needs to be accomplished in order to pursue your organization's mission.

Here's an example of a mission statement of a car parts seller that wants to dominate the market in its area. *"To become the top auto parts retailer in North America, by providing first-class customer value and care."* The firm has set out its goal and the primary means by which it aims to achieve it. The goal included is quantifiable. That is, the firm will be able to see by industry comparison whether it's approaching its goal and if it has been reached.

The statement is also appropriate as it aligns with the seller's intent to dominate the market in its area. It sets out that intention and how it will be achieved.

Similarly, the mission statement is specific in how the company has decided to become the market leader, by differentiating itself from competitors in terms of value and the level of service it provides.

Contrast the previous mission statement with this one for a medical wholesaler that aims to be a leading supplier in its field. *"To provide access to medical equipment and supplies for private facilities and public institutions, inspiring the public, and creating sustainable shareholder growth going forward."* This statement provides no quantifiable objective – there would be no figures the firm could examine to see if its mission is being fulfilled.

This statement isn't appropriate as it deviates from the vision of the company, or, at the very least, it fails to explain it properly. You might wonder if this was a mission statement for a charity or for a corporation if it weren't for the inclusion of shareholder growth.

The statement also isn't specific enough in stating how the company's mission will be fulfilled. While terms like "inspiring" sound good, they don't make it clear what actions should be taken.

As well as being well-defined, a high-performing organization's mission statement also provides a consistent focal point for employees' action. It helps align leader, manager, and employee action with the organization's strategy and underlying philosophy. Everyone sees how their role helps the organization achieve its goals.

Here's the mission statement of a restaurant chain:

"Ensuring that each customer receives quick, cordial, professional, and courteous service. Providing, at a reasonable price, healthy meals, using high-quality ingredients."

This mission statement sets out what is expected of employees and hence has a consistent focal point for employees' action. It sets out their role in relation to the customer and what level of service they're expected to provide.

It also lays out the strategic direction of management. As per the statement, the restaurant must seek good value ingredients where it can, without sacrificing the quality of ingredients.

When writing your mission statement it may be beneficial to consult with employees. When you incorporate their input, you're more likely to create a mission statement they'll stand by and have a greater interest in fulfilling.

You could create an informal employee survey in order to get feedback from all quarters on how your organization's mission should be defined. If possible, you could even get feedback from customers with regard to your mission statement.

Although mission statements vary in length, they should be, if possible, written so that they can be easily memorized by staff members. This makes it easier for employees to refer back to the mission statement for guidance. A great mission statement may not only guide your employees, but also inspire them to greater work.

For example, management at an Asian communications startup decides to consult staff members on what they think their mission statement should entail. Suggestion forms are sent around to staff members, and meetings are held to discuss the statement's formulation.

A draft mission statement comes out of the consultation:

"To become Asia's premier communications logistics, delivery, and solutions experts. We'll do this through being of a constant innovative

mindset, specializing in locale-specific bespoke communications developments."

The statement is deemed too long and hard to memorize. It's rewritten to be shorter and more easily memorized.

"To become Asia's premier communications solutions experts, through constant locale-specific research."

A strong mission statement sets out in well-defined terms the purpose of the organization, its prospects for the future, and it also provides a focus to clarify employees' positions within the organization. A well- written mission statement can even serve to inspire customers and attract prospective employees. For example, here's a travel agency's mission statement: *"Continuously improving our customers' travel experiences through 24/7 care and support; to become the premier travel company in Europe."*

Measuring performance

High-performing organizations are underpinned by flexible and attainable strategic plans. High- performing strategic plans focus on internal strategy but balance it with a flexible attitude to external factors. If the circumstances change beyond the organization, the organization can also change to best exploit the new situation. A robust strategic plan includes a realistic assessment of where the organization currently stands, as well as a description of its goals and how they'll be achieved.

Strategic plans should include methods for measuring performance, detailed in an appraisal program. This enables you to evaluate whether the plan is being implemented effectively and whether it's bringing benefit to the organization. These measurements can help encourage focus and clarity across the organization. However, to be useful, the performance metrics should be clearly defined from the outset.

Performance measurement for high-performing organizations requires three core facets. First, performance measures must be clearly defined. Second, when performance measures are put in place, they must measure the right things. And third, performance measures should include benchmarks, timelines, and consequences for failure to meet quantifiables. All of these should be included in your appraisal program.

Be clearly defined

When performance measures are clearly defined, employees have a better sense of what's expected of them. They'll also see where they can improve personal performance. If the measures are undefined, it becomes difficult to compare metrics on a like-for-like basis. This also makes it difficult to analyze long-term trends.

Measure the right things

If you're not measuring the right things, you won't be able to improve the right performance areas. What aspects of your organization you choose to measure depends on what areas have the most room for improvement and are most integral to your organization's high performance.

Benchmarks, timelines, and consequences

As your organization strives to become high-performing, it's important that it's clear to all involved what's expected in terms of objectives, timescale, and improvement. Staff members must know what management expects of them and generally all employees should know what's expected of each other. Detailing consequences for failure to meet quantifiables motivates employees to go that extra mile to achieve high performance.

Clear definition is essential to performance measurement. Setting out objectives that are ill-defined may cause conflict among those tasked to fulfill them.

Basic performance measures relate to cost and efficiency. So your strategic plan might set out where improvements should be made with regard to output.

Your plan might include the objective "Unit costs to be lowered 10% in the coming year," which is a clearly defined area of performance that can be measured. Measuring performance shouldn't just monitor whether this target is met; it should include processes by which improvements can be made.

Sales volume, product quality, customer service, sales targets, employee morale, and innovation are other areas where you'll want high-performance and where performance is measurable. Non-profit organizations have other criteria such as, in the case of charities, response times, fundraising, or inter-organizational cooperation, where performance could be higher.

Your appraisal program could include the objective *"Client satisfaction must be improved by reducing customer complaints by 75% this quarter."* Again, this is a clearly defined objective, and one that's measurable by conducting regular client surveys.

In contrast, the objective "Elevate workplace synergy to achieve optimum interpersonal efficiencies" isn't clearly defined. It would be difficult to measure whether this objective had been achieved.

The performance measures your appraisal program sets out should measure the right things. There are a number of metrics that could be used to measure the performance of your organization, depending on which aspects of it you want to improve.

If you want to emphasize customer service, then performance measures that check customer satisfaction would be the most appropriate. For instance, although sales measures would give you a rough indication of customer satisfaction, they don't clearly show whether customer service is improving.

Similarly, if you were measuring how much interdepartmental communication had improved, tallying the patents filed in your company's name would be of little or no benefit. However, tallying the volume of calls, faxes, and e-mails between departments would give clear indicators of communication.

The final aspect of performance measurement for high-performing organizations relates to imparting what's expected of your staff members. Benchmarks, timelines, and consequences of failure to meet quantifiables all communicate clearly to your staff members what must be achieved and what's at stake. Benchmarks are the objectives that must be achieved. Timelines are the allotted time in which they must be achieved. And the consequences are what will happen if objectives aren't achieved.

Benchmarks for performance might be laid out, for example, in terms of projected growth or improvements. An example would include, *"Monthly sales should increase 5%."*

Timelines for performance would be included, setting out what time period performance will be measured in, such as *"Monthly sales should increase 5% in the next four quarters."*

The consequences of failure could be set out in terms of future prospects and bonuses called into question if targets aren't met, for example *"Monthly sales should increase 5% in the next four quarters. If target is not met, salesperson bonuses may not be awarded."*

Performance measures are tools that aid our understanding of what our organizations actually do, and they provide insights into how to improve them. Key to attaining high performance, measurements should be clear from the outset in terms of what you're seeking to improve, and how you'll measure that improvement.

Customer focus

Communicating regularly with customers is an essential strategy for any high-performing organization. Using customer input enables you to create better value for both your customers and your organization. Your organization has complete control over how it interacts with its customers. However, you have little control over some other factors that influence how customers interact with your organization. These factors include global competition, regulations, the pace of change, and technology.

There are three means by which a high-performing organization can maintain effective customer focus. First, your organization needs to have clear approaches to customer recruitment, satisfaction, and commitment. Second, you should align your strategy to achieve value for your customers. And finally, you should ensure your employees understand customer needs and expectations, and know how their work contributes to customer service.

Your organization needs to have clearly set out approaches to customer recruitment, satisfaction, and commitment. A plan should be made that details the processes by which your organization attracts new customers, how it interacts with current customers, and how it will retain their customers in the future.

Brand differentiation, marketing, and other methods can be used to attract customers to your organization. Ongoing customer service and technical support should also be in place so that customers remain satisfied with your organization beyond just the immediate products and services they purchase.

High-performing organizations consider customer information such as feedback, sales trends, and other indicators when developing new products and services. They also accurately anticipate their customers' longer-term needs. High-performing organizations ultimately strive to become premier value providers, exceeding customers' expectations.

Aligning strategy to achieve value for customers is crucial. Your organization should excel at the things that provide customer value. To do this, you must know your customers and understand what their specific needs are. You can then devise a strategy that creates the most value for your customers and fosters customer loyalty.

High-performing organizations have ongoing communication with their customers. They discover what their customers need and decide which of these needs they can meet. They then design products or services that create the most value for both parties.

By collaborating with your customers, your organization can build value, increase customer retention, and devise better products and services that will be popular with future customers.

In order to be customer focused, high-performing organizations must also ensure that employees understand customer needs and expectations and know how their work contributes to customer service. Employees, especially those in regular contact with customers, need to know how their roles feed in to customer service. They should understand what customers need. You should seek feedback from customers about employees' customer service skills, and use this feedback to help improve employees' interactions with customers.

High-performing leadership

Leadership is another important feature of a high-performing organization. Leaders have many roles to play in an organization. They're goal setters and motivators, coaches and mentors, interpreters, coordinators, and visionaries. Ultimately, leaders should cultivate employees, setting clear goals for them, understanding their individual abilities, and guiding their performance. High-performing leaders embody all these roles and more.

Goal setters and motivators

Leaders direct and motivate employees toward achieving objectives, correctly and promptly. They spend time with employees, communicating the purpose of objectives that are set for them.

Coaches and mentors

Leaders know employees want to improve and learn. They also know that employees will want to contribute more to the organization, given the right chances and incentives.

Interpreters

Leaders explain situations where there's not enough information available, or when guidelines and plans for making decisions and taking action may not exist.

Coordinators

Leaders need to coordinate all the different groups of individuals within an organization to ensure they work together effectively.

Visionaries

Leaders must be able to imagine the future and encourage employees to be positive about change. They must be able to quickly adapt their organizations to constant change.

There are three main practices that are characteristic of high-performing leadership. The first is achieving a balance between showing concern for people and showing concern for task issues. The second is coaching and managing clear expectations for employees. And the third is focusing on larger objectives, not the small details of the business. To be a high-performing leader, you should be adept at each of these.

The first practice of high-performing leadership is achieving a balance between showing concern for people and showing concern for task issues. Leaders are often focused on one concern or another, but they should be flexible in their approach so as to lead people effectively.

Often, leaders are more concerned with what must be done, not with how it's done. However, occasionally circumstances may demand closer attention on their part. Sometimes leaders must allow their employees to take the reins to a degree, whereas in other instances, a more controlling approach is required.

Some leaders treat their relationship with employees like a formal transaction. Employees are told what to do, and then they do it and are rewarded for doing it well. Once staff members are obedient, the leader is

satisfied. Other leaders look beyond compliance, seeking commitment from employees. They
establish personal relationships with employees and quiz them on their needs and their ideas, helping them perform better. They know they can't lead in isolation, so they build a rapport with those they lead.

For example, a financial firm's leader, Chen, finds that two staff members are in conflict over an issue that is delaying a major project's completion. Focusing on the task, Chen orders them to resolve the issue promptly, or face disciplinary action. The project is put back on track. However, the underlying causes of the conflict aren't addressed. This is storing problems for the future.

Later, trouble arises again between the staff members, with personal insults having been exchanged. Chen, realizing his first approach wasn't entirely successful, tries a different approach. He calls together the staff members in a candid meeting and asks them to talk through their issues. They soon resolve the issues, permanently. In this instance, concern for people yields the best result for the organization.

The second aspect of high-performance leadership is coaching and managing clear expectations for employees. Sometimes employees need to be coached. Instead of just giving orders to your employees, you should cultivate their abilities and encourage them to develop their skills. Make clear to employees what is expected of them within the organization.

Effective leaders treat employees respectfully, knowing they can improve and learn, and if given the right opportunities and rewards, they will want to help create a better organization. Leaders who get to know employees as individuals often reward them for good work. They don't resort to punishment when mistakes are made. Instead, they use those situations as learning opportunities.

Without guidance as to what is expected of them, employees may never reach their full potential within an organization. In order to do the job right, they need to know what is expected of them.

Consider the differing leadership styles of Andrea and Shawna. They both lead teams in an electronics factory. Andrea's style is very hands-off. Some of the new staff members are unhappy, as a lot of things haven't been explained to them. Although they know their precise jobs in the factory setup, they've no idea what's expected of them in terms of productivity. This uncertainty is putting an instant dent in their morale.

In contrast, Shawna makes time to have a personal talk with each new employee. She makes sure the employees know their role in the factory and what is expected of them in the long term. She makes clear to employees that if they have concerns, they are welcome to voice them. Employees appreciate the clarity Shawna's style brings, and overall, are a more satisfied and more effective group of workers than Andrea's team.

The third hallmark of high-performing leadership is focusing on larger objectives, not the minor details. In a busy organization, any number of tasks may be occurring at the same time. Leaders can't and shouldn't supervise every single thing that occurs within the organization.

Effective leaders must make broad plans and coordinate the activities of the disparate individuals under their leadership. Although occasionally specific issues may merit detailed attention, generally leaders shouldn't be involved in the day-to-day activities of the organization but should always be working for and planning for the long term.

For example, Pierre is a leader in an insurance company. He allocates the office supplies budget for the coming year. He doesn't decide what this budget is spent on, nor will he be ordering these supplies. This level of attention isn't feasible, especially in larger corporations.

High-performing culture

Every organization has its own internal culture. An organization's culture encompasses the shared values, norms, and beliefs of its employees. These shared assumptions shape what actions and strategic options are considered within the organization. To make yours a high-performing organization, you must ensure that a culture exists that's conducive to high-performance.

In order to build a high-performing organization, you need to foster a culture that will give it a competitive advantage. Your organization's culture should align with its strategic mission and with the external environment, while differentiating itself from competitors. However, the culture has to be flexible in order to adapt to changing circumstances beyond the organization. The ability to adapt quickly is crucial to maintaining an edge over rivals.

All organizations have a culture. In some instances, however, a corporate culture can hinder the organization by being too rigid, resistant to change, and by maintaining working methods that have outlived their usefulness.

In high-performing organizations, managers usually take deliberate steps to influence how the culture is formed. They can help shape a culture through their actions and words, espousing the organization's values, and displaying those values in their actions.

Organizational culture is something that managers can guide but can never fully control. For every aspect of the culture that you can adjust or influence, there are other aspects that are beyond your power to change.

However, those factors that you do have control over can be manipulated to contribute to your organization's success.

Remember, every employee in your organization contributes to its culture. Employees should be given the tools and the encouragement to work toward both personal and organizational high performance. Your employees should feel they have a personal stake in how well your organization succeeds. They should also feel a personal responsibility for staying abreast of changes both within and outside the organization.

You may have noted that the culture should encourage people to excel. In fact, there are five primary characteristics of a high-performing culture. The culture fosters a mentality where individuals want to

excel. It's also built around clearly-defined strategic goals. Another characteristic is that it reflects and accommodates external factors. Also, employees have some autonomy. The final characteristic of a high-performing culture is that open communication prevails.

A high-performing culture fosters a mentality where individuals want to excel. It fosters an environment where employees don't just comply with orders; they commit to the organization. They feel they have a stake in, and responsibility for, the organization's success, and for fulfilling its strategy. They understand that their personal success is linked to the overall success of the organization.

Managers in a company might steer the company's culture toward recognizing individual successes, but with an emphasis on the fact that everyone benefits. Awarding certificates, or some other informal tokens, when targets are met or exceeded may help foster the desired mentality. For example, managers might institute a Teammate of the Month program.

Other activities that may help create a mentality where individuals want to excel include team-building exercises and lectures from renowned high performers. Similarly, managers can talk informally to each employee about the company's goals and their own goals and how these intersect.

It's important that a high-performing culture is built around a clearly-defined strategic goal or goals. Your company's culture should be geared toward fulfilling goals as set out in your strategy and mission.

Everyone within the organization must be reminded of what they should be doing, and why they're doing it. Sometimes when organizations expand or diversify, their culture can lose sight of what it is that they set out to achieve and how they initially differentiated themselves from others.

For example, a car manufacturer's mission may initially have been to produce high-quality vehicles, but with competition it might find itself in a price war with lower cost rivals. This might steer the company's culture away from its initial mission and toward cost-cutting, which is often incompatible with high-quality production. The company might convene a conference where its initial mission is reaffirmed to employees at all levels.

In order to maintain a competitive edge, an organization's culture must reflect and accommodate external factors. These include competition, consumer tastes, technology, and regulations. These factors may change over time and your organization's culture will have to adapt to that change or risk irrelevance.

Being able to accommodate changed circumstances quickly is one of the best advantages your organization can have over rivals. If your company's culture is geared toward providing a product or service that the public is starting to lose interest in, you would have to steer your culture to better align with public taste.

Consider a cosmetics company, for example. Suppose new regulations prohibit the use of key components in the company's products. The company would have to change its products and its culture in order to ensure it complies with the changing regulations. The culture would have to encourage employees to keep up to date with the changing products.

Another characteristic of a high-performing organizational culture is allowing employees to have some autonomy. Managers can't manage everything. When a culture is geared toward the organization's strategy, employees can be left to make some decisions on their own. Encouraging some decision making when dealing with customers, for example, can help the employee quickly satisfy the customer without wasting time consulting superiors. Also, employees might be better positioned to make good decisions when dealing with day-to-day problems.

The final characteristic of a high-performance culture is that open communication prevails in the organization. Personal communication is important within an organization. Effective managers get to know their employees personally, establishing relationships with each.

Top-down communication should be accompanied by employee-to-manager communication. Managers should actively listen to employees, collaborating to discuss new ideas, commitment, and enthusiasm. In effect, the other four characteristics couldn't exist without this one because open communication makes all the other characteristics more likely.

There are numerous ways managers can foster a communication culture. Encouraging employees to schedule meetings with managers or implementing regular round-table discussions of organizational issues can help. Similarly, employees can be encouraged to fill out suggestion forms to be reviewed by managers.

There are some organizational cultures that actively resist high performance. In some companies, managers may exercise too much control over everything, damaging employee morale and productivity with, for example, constant and harsh performance reviews. They may actively discourage employees from doing anything other than precisely what they're told to do, no more and no less. Compliant employees may make for an adequate organization, but without employee commitment, an organization may never reach high performance and will eventually fall prey to rivals.

For example, a secretarial services company has a culture that works against employee satisfaction and autonomy. The prominently placed motto, "The nail that sticks out gets hammered down," indicates management attitudes to employee initiative. The culture actively dampens employee morale. The work gets done, but the company doesn't progress, innovate, or grow to the extent it could.

Staff members know their services aren't as good as they could be, and they have numerous ideas for how they can be improved. The managers won't listen to employees' suggestions and scoff at the idea of regular manager and employee discussions.

Consequently the managers are out of touch, and they are very slow to react to changed circumstances outside the company. The way things are done hasn't changed in years. The current culture doesn't really fit the company's original mission: to create new and fast secretarial services.

In contrast, at an IT firm, staff members are encouraged to do their work as best they can and are rewarded for their accomplishments. The company's culture is geared toward constant innovation, which is a primary objective of the firm's mission.

The culture is outward looking, the fast-changing IT world is observed, analyzed, and adjusted to within the firm's culture. Employees are encouraged to take some control over what fields of innovation they choose to operate in.

Finally, the managers have a system in place where staff members are encouraged to suggest new ideas and problems, and make other comments to management, without fear of repercussions.

Learning Aid - **Balancing Organizational Factors**

There are several internal aspects and external factors that must be balanced in an organization when striving to achieve high performance.

Internal factors	External elements
Strategy and mission	Available talent
Structures and processes	Global competition
Customer orientation	Faster and more disruptive change
Leadership	Technology
Organizational culture	Political and regulatory changes
	Influence of ethics
	Environmental factors

Learning Aid - Characteristics of High-performance Culture

Competitive advantage can be found through gearing your organization to high-performance. Making sure your culture is properly calibrated is one thing you can do to ensure your company achieves and maintains high-performance.

Characteristic of High-performance Culture	Explanation
Fostering a mentality where individuals want to excel	Individuals want to commit to the organization, not just comply. Individuals realize that individual success is tied in with organizational success.
Culture is based around clearly defined strategic goals	The culture should be calibrated towards the fulfillment of the organization's mission.
Culture reflects and accommodates external factors	The culture must align with and adapt to ever-changing external factors such as competition, customer demand, technology, and regulation.
Employees have some autonomy	An organization can work more effectively if employees can make some decisions without consulting managers. It empowers employees but also makes them better at their work.
Open communication prevails	One-to-one communication between managers and employees is essential. Employees should be encouraged to voice their concerns and ideas for the organization.

Learning Aid - Management Types

You can print this document, or re-create the table in a word processing or spreadsheet application and use it to complete this activity.

Think about the roles you perform as a leader. Which management type do you think fits you best? Going through the list of management types, award yourself points for each, as follows:

1 – "I fit this type well"
2 – "I fit this type OK, but there's probably room for improvement"
3 – "I don't fit this type well, and really want to improve this

Use the end result as a reminder of ways in which you would like to improve as a leader going forward.

Management Type	Points
Goal-setter and motivator	
Coach and mentor	
Interpreter	
Coordinator	
Visionary	

CHAPTER TWO
Cross-Functional Strategic Management

Cross-Functional Strategic Management
Cross-functional management, or CFM, is the management of business processes across functional boundaries. It consists of managers working together to support the organization's goals. It manages functions to create synergy, provides leadership that synergizes expertise, and adopts a horizontal and vertical outlook.

CFM minimizes sub-optimization, improves creativity, allows the free flow of information and, ultimately, puts the focus on the customer.

Many companies are implementing cross-functional management structures to meet business challenges. Four principles apply when implementing a strategic cross-functional initiative: First, try to strike a balance and blend top-down and bottom-up orientations. Second, develop a cross-functional culture so that all employees understand how their work impacts others. Third, define goals clearly. And finally, communicate appropriately to encourage collaboration.

Knowledge management is conducive to cross-functionality because it helps to overcome organizational silos, fosters solutions that benefit the entire organization, supports knowledge sharing, and encourages the organization to unify around common goals.

Many organizations have found that knowledge management approaches – communities of practice, knowledge repositories, action reviews, and best practice replication – are the best ways to enhance organizational cross-functionality.

Cross-functional management
Every day, organizations face a fast-changing business environment that's global and competitive. To continue to grow, some organizations adapt themselves to become more cross-functional. They're taking

advantage of the flexibility of this new structure to help them respond to these business challenges.

Cross-functionality involves bringing together people with diverse talents from different departments to achieve a common goal.

Cross-functional organizations adapt themselves by interweaving functional activities. Each cross- function involves several departments and is typically guided by one or more senior managers.

Cross-functional management, or CFM, is the management of business processes across functional boundaries. It consists of managers working together to support the organization's goals. CFM achieves this by building processes and systems to foster organizational change in areas such as innovation, quality, cost, and customer satisfaction.

CFM is a management process centered on open communication and cooperation. It has been adopted by leading manufacturers like Toyota Motor Corporation and Hewlett-Packard.

CFM has a number of characteristics:
- it manages across functions to achieve organizational synergy
- it provides leadership to synergize different areas of expertise, and
- It adopts both a horizontal and a vertical outlook

Managing across functions means coordinating functions as a way of creating synergy to support business operations. Consider this example. An aircraft manufacturer appoints a VP as cross-functional manager to coordinate testing across the Engineering, Assembly, and Test Departments. The goal is to find ways to reduce testing time.

Providing leadership in cross-functional organizations is key to being able to capitalize on functional expertise. To enable specialists to make the greatest contribution, you should show them how their expertise fits into, and supports, the organization's goals.

A cross-functional manager should have a working knowledge of the technical issues. This means knowing enough about the various subject areas to understand issues and follow discussions.

In addition, the cross-functional manager needs the interpersonal skills to lead a diverse group. The manager should be highly skilled in such areas as conflict resolution, consensus building, and people management.

The vice-president (VP) appointed to coordinate test activities at the aircraft manufacturer knows enough about test techniques to lead, direct, and motivate a team of people from different departments to achieve the goal. Within six months, the team has come up with revolutionary new test methods that reduce testing time for new aircraft by three weeks.

Functional management aims to optimize the performance of a specific function. CFM, on the other hand, adopts both a horizontal and vertical outlook. The intent is to create synergies in both directions.

Some problems cross the entire organization. A management approach that represents all points of view is the best approach to solving such problems and preventing new ones.

Following on from the success in reducing aircraft test time, the VP wants to introduce the new test methods across the company. To do this, the VP uses the talents of the Communications and Marketing Departments to spread the message about the new test methods across all departments. The VP also ensures that all organizational levels are aligned with the new test methods.

Benefits of cross-functional management

If you think of an organization as being like an orchestra where each department is a different instrument, you can see why CFM is so valuable. A cross-functional manager is like the conductor who ensures that all instruments or departments are in harmony.

Functional organizations face challenges when they try to execute projects that need a cross-functional approach:

There's limited internal integration among functions, such as development and marketing, with a consequent risk of disconnects between them.
- There's limited external integration among key stakeholders such as customers or suppliers.
- There's poor business process execution across functions.
- Sometimes, key deliverables are rushed, or missed entirely. This leads to serious issues – for example requirement gaps found late in a project's development cycle.
- There's a lack of information sharing.
- There can be a lack of focus, due to confused responsibility.
- The message can get distorted when individuals attempt to communicate across functions.
- There's resistance to change.
- There's little opportunity for organizational learning.

Consider this example. A computer manufacturer with a functional organizational structure has designed and developed a new laptop.

However, when the laptop is launched, the Sales Department realizes that several key features are missing. A root cause analysis reveals that a lack of coordination between Marketing and Engineering caused requirements to be left out of the product.

Customers are also reporting reliability problems with the laptop's hard disk drive. Again, an analysis shows that Engineering did not specify the correct disk type when sourcing components from an external supplier.

CFM has four specific advantages for organizations. It minimizes suboptimization, enhances creativity and innovation, promotes information sharing, and puts the focus where it should be – on the customer.

CFM minimizes suboptimization by managing business processes across functional boundaries. suboptimization occurs when a benefit for a function harms the organization as a whole.

Consider this example. The director of manufacturing in a bus manufacturing company is to coordinate efforts of the R&D, Manufacturing, and QA Departments to reduce defects. The director and his team review all the aspects of component assembly.

The team discovers that a plastic component, introduced to lower the weight of the final assembly, is subject to excessive wear. The team replaces the suboptimized component with a stronger metal equivalent. The result is that defects are reduced by 20%.

The second benefit of CFM is that it enhances creativity and innovation by bringing together people with different experiences. This stimulates creativity and fresh thinking. In such an environment, with its mix of experiences, new ideas can emerge.

The bus manufacturer has noted an increase in defects during testing. The director of manufacturing directs his team to resolve the issue.

Using their diverse skills, the team members discover that most testing is carried out in final assembly. They recommend that each critical subcomponent be tested before assembly.

The team discovers that a plastic component, introduced to lower the weight of the final assembly, is subject to excessive wear. The team replaces the suboptimized component with a stronger metal equivalent. The result is that defects are reduced by 20%.

The second benefit of CFM is that it enhances creativity and innovation by bringing together people with different experiences. This stimulates creativity and fresh thinking. In such an environment, with its mix of experiences, new ideas can emerge.

The bus manufacturer has noted an increase in defects during testing. The director of manufacturing directs his team to resolve the issue.

Using their diverse skills, the team members discover that most testing is carried out in final assembly. They recommend that each critical subcomponent be tested before assembly.

The fourth benefit of CFM is that it puts the focus on the customer. Because the cross-functional organization is able to work in collaboration on the big picture, it can focus on the objective of serving the customer.

In the case of the bus manufacturing company, knowledge and experience mean that the team knows enough to fully understand the delivery process, identify potential issues, reduce errors, and, ultimately, deliver quality to the customer.

Cross-functional organizations also improve customer focus by providing a single point of contact. In functional organizations, it's often difficult to know who to go to for definitive information when working on a complex project.

Orientation and culture

To survive and compete, many organizations are developing cross-functional structures. They recognize how the strengths and flexibility of this new structure can help them respond to business challenges.

There are two approaches you can take to develop a cross-functional organization: top down and bottom up. The top-down approach begins with top-level management defining an organizational vision. Management then states a mission and a strategy to deliver on that mission. Employees then take concrete actions based on these. The bottom-up approach takes the reverse path. It means that there is active employee input in setting goals and strategies. Each approach has its advantages and drawbacks.

The top-down approach has the advantage of consistency. Setting goals at the top and distributing them down through the organization means that all goals are based on one overall goal.

The top-down approach allows goals to be based on key stakeholders' views of the business and the competition, giving goals a sound commercial footing. Finally, the top-down approach allows top-level expectations to be clearly communicated to each participant.

Consider this example. A newspaper editor formulates a high-level goal for a new online magazine. The goal is restated, in a top-down manner, for each level in the organization so that assistant editors and journalists understand their part in delivering the goal.

One disadvantage you may have noted is that lower-level managers aren't empowered to take the initiative based on their experience. Another disadvantage is that goals handed down from above may not be recognized as being relevant to those working on lower levels. This might result in reduced productivity. In addition, top management may drive goals that would be better driven at lower levels. Finally, employees may not understand or accept goals, and therefore aren't motivated to deliver on them.

Consider this example. The CEO of a software vendor outlines a new goal of making the company's graphics software available on cloud computing platforms.

The new goal is communicated throughout the organization.

But because the goal is stated at such a high level, people in lower levels in the organization don't know what to do to deliver on the goal.

The bottom-up approach has a number of advantages. First, the planning process speeds up because it's simplified by taking the right input from a number of different people. For example, action lists from different people could be used as input to a project plan.

Second, the whole organization is involved in setting strategic direction, which makes buy-in more likely.

Finally, the approach encourages individuals to think creatively, which tends to produce more imaginative and successful ways of implementing the strategy.

The bottom-up approach does have some disadvantages, though. It can lack clarity, accountability, and control because teams formulate their own plans.

Consider this example. The executive team at a bank uses the bottom-up approach to plan financial targets. Each function within the bank formulates its own plan on how it will contribute to meeting the targets.

However, in the planning process, no function is made accountable for meeting the overall targets. The result is that at the end of the year, the bank fails to meet its financial targets.

Blending orientations

There are four principles that will help you implement strategic cross-functionality in your organization: blend top-down and bottom-up orientations, develop a cross-functional culture, define goals clearly, and communicate appropriately.

As with many aspects of organizational development, the best approach is to strike a balance. In this case, it's a good idea to blend top-down and bottom-up orientations. You should take those aspects of both approaches that suit your organization's strategies and avoid those aspects that cause problems.

A common approach is to drive strategy from the top down but to execute strategy from the bottom up so that it permeates the whole organization.

When considering which approach to take, you should take a cross-functional view, act collaboratively, and gather input from all levels of the organization to successfully implement your approach.

Consider this example. The CEO of an airline decides to use the blended approach to set the company strategy for the next three years.

The executive team formulates the overall strategy. This is because the team is familiar with the competition and regulatory issues.

On the other hand, mid-level managers plan and execute the strategy. This is because they know how the business operates on the ground.

Developing a cross-functional culture

You can also support cross-functionality by developing a cross-functional culture. A truly cross- functional organizational culture is one where all employees understand how their work impacts others. They also understand how they contribute to reaching organizational goals.

Many companies see the value in developing cross-functional knowledge. For example, consider Toyota Motor Corporation.

In Toyota's culture, everyone knows how roles feed into the company's strategic goals. There's mutual support between functional areas in the effort to reach a common goal.

Organizational culture is often difficult to change and it will likely take time and effort. For example, as part of the organizational culture there might be a collective emphasis on deadlines. While meeting deadlines is important, it might distract from the organizational objectives.

To place focus back on the customer, you need to encourage a culture of sharing and interdependence that focuses on the needs of the customer.

Mid-level and senior-level managers shape an organization's culture. But managers don't act alone; it's professionals across all functions who bring the culture to life. However, managers can develop a cross- functional culture by providing leadership, communicating vision and values, facilitating knowledge sharing, and encouraging continuous improvement.

Providing leadership

To provide leadership, senior managers should have good communication skills so that all employees can understand the objectives and benefits of the cross-functional initiative.

Communicating vision and values

Managers should ensure each individual knows the organization's goals and objectives and how individuals contribute to them.

Facilitating knowledge sharing

To bring a cross-functional culture to all corners of the organization, managers should facilitate open communication of ideas, experiences, and knowledge.

Encouraging continuous improvement

Managers should encourage ideas for continuous improvement from all functions and levels.

To provide leadership, senior managers should direct, communicate, and most important, model the cross-functional culture.

For example, suppose an insurance company wants to create a cross-functional culture. To help achieve this, the CEO defines customer needs as one of the company's core values. The senior managers might model the culture change by spending two hours a week working as customer support agents.

Having face-to-face, real-time interactions in a meeting or presentation is the best way for senior managers to communicate a cultural vision and its values.

Imagine the case of the CEO of the insurance company who wants to ensure that the message about customer needs is fully understood by all employees.

She could set up a program of meetings where senior executives deliver the message to employees at every branch office. Each presentation might include a question and answer session where employees can raise concerns.

You should adopt a culture that facilitates knowledge sharing. This ensures that information flows freely among seniority levels and functional units. This extends beyond the company to suppliers, dealers, and even customers.

You should develop, implement, and adhere to a continuous improvement program. And you should encourage your employees to follow it. Some companies continually change their improvement programs to reflect the latest trends. It's hard to improve when the program changes all the time.

You should initiate cultural change from the top down, but everyone from the bottom up must be involved in the change. This approach includes training in team building and problem solving. Finally, your middle managers should drive transformation.

Defining goals clearly

The third principle when developing cross-functionality is that you should define goals clearly. To perform to their potential, cross-functional organizations need to have both a clear understanding of the goal and a belief that achieving the goal is important to the organization.

You should set clear goals for the organization. These should be stated at a high level but should also support a common objective for the organization. For example, a goal stating the need to improve quality applies to many functions but also supports the overall objective of improving customer satisfaction.

Your goal should define the problem that needs to be solved, not the solution that needs to be achieved. Also, when setting goals, determine if there are any operating limits. For example – are there time or budget limitations?

Finally, you should identify key functional interdependencies. Does one function have to complete a task before another can begin?

Clear goals are particularly important for organizations pursuing cross-functionality. You should set clear goals for the organization that are high level but that support a common objective.

Greater interaction across traditional functional boundaries creates potential for conflict. Clear goals can reduce these risks by giving a sense of shared purpose. The goal needs to be seen as valuable and clear.

Goals should recognize and leverage the expertise within the organization. They should be broad enough to allow all to play their parts and work collaboratively.

Here's an example of a clear goal at work at an Internet service provider.

The executive team at the Internet service provider sets a goal to "halve turnaround time for creating online customer accounts within three months." The goal is communicated across all functions and at all levels within the organization.

Within six months, the CEO judges the goal to be achieved. This is because the goal is clearly stated at a high level, it doesn't prescribe a solution, it includes relevant constraints, and, most important, everyone in the company understands the importance of the goal.

Communicating appropriately

The fourth principle when developing a cross-functional approach is to communicate appropriately. This helps to ensure that your strategy is accepted across the organization. When deciding how to communicate, you need to take account of inter-functional politics.

Cross-functional structures are made up of people from different organizational units. They may have competing loyalties and feel obliged to support their functional areas. For instance, a production team might be so focused on meeting its own production targets that it loses sight of high-level quality objectives set by the organization.

There may have been past difficulties between people in functions which may cause problems. Additionally, people may think that their functional area should take precedence over other areas.

CEOs and high-level managers should communicate appropriately by stating goals clearly, encouraging harmony and collaboration, and ensuring everyone knows where they fit in the operation so that territorial issues are avoided.

The best way to reduce the effect of negative politics and avoid conflict is by communicating goals clearly.

Organizational goals should be interpreted and restated at each level so that each person knows how to contribute to achieving the overall goal.

Cross-functional structures can cause tension. Open communication can ease this tension by encouraging harmony and collaboration within the organization.

This requires more effort than, for example, working collaboratively during a meeting. For short-term activities, it might be enough for the existing work methods to be temporarily put aside.

But creating a culture of harmonious collaboration requires people to change their behavior to support collaboration.

You need to ensure everyone knows where they fit in the operation and how they contribute to the organization's goals. Poorly defined roles and responsibilities can result in confusion, duplication, and gaps in responsibilities because the definition of who does what is vague.

Communicating to avoid territorial issues requires you to draw and communicate clear lines so that functional units know where their responsibilities begin and end.

Consider this example. The executive team at an IT vendor outlines a strategy for delivering software on time and within budget. However, the CEO is careful to assign the task of delivering on budget to the financial director and the task of delivering on quality to the engineering director.

Managing knowledge

What do you think would be the response if you were to ask CEOs from five different companies how to support a cross-functional strategy in their organization? You would most likely get five different answers.

Some ways of supporting a cross-functional organization are to blend top-down and bottom-up orientations, develop a cross-functional culture, and use appropriate communication.

But having these structures in place isn't enough – systems that support cross-functional business operations are also crucial. A knowledge management system is one such tool.

Implementing knowledge management systems is the easy part. Companies also need to create the environment, culture, and processes to encourage people to share what they know. This involves getting employees to share their knowledge and experiences.

To create valuable knowledge, people need to access and understand data from previous projects. They then need to interpret this data so that they can identify patterns and predict future events.

For example, an IT director analyzes data from three software releases and sees that faults have increased with every release. The director then institutes a root cause analysis and traces the problem to inadequate release testing procedures.

Conversely, gathering knowledge without being able to access, share, or capture value from it is wasteful.

Knowledge management can be thought of in a number of ways. It's a way of structuring what the organization knows, it's about creating the right environment to promote the dissemination of knowledge, and it's about designing processes for collecting and using knowledge.

Structuring what the organization knows

Knowledge management is a way of structuring what the organization knows so that the organization's knowledge can be used to teach, learn, and create value for the organization, its employees, and its customers.

Creating the right environment

Knowledge management should be about creating and sustaining an environment that enables the creation, dissemination, and uptake of the organization's knowledge.

Designing processes

Knowledge management is about designing processes that collect, format, and structure knowledge so that it's available for reuse throughout the organization.

There's no standard method for knowledge management. Depending on your organization's requirements, you need to work out a framework involving the three elements: knowledge categories, knowledge processes, and knowledge enablers.

The first knowledge category is tacit knowledge. This is knowledge that's difficult to transfer to another person – for example the ability to use a programming language to create a web browser. This requires knowledge that isn't always known explicitly.

The second knowledge category is explicit knowledge. This is knowledge that can be easily recorded, transmitted, and understood by a recipient – for example the fact that the head of a company is called a CEO.

The third knowledge category is cultural knowledge. This is knowledge gained from experience – for example a salesperson's knowledge of customers' buying habits and preferences.

The first knowledge process is knowledge creation, which is achieved through experience. For example, after a sales manager creates a sales spreadsheet, the sales VP notes on the spreadsheet that some products have reduced sales – this is information. The VP then uses competitor information and judgment to conclude that some products are overpriced.

In this case, knowledge has been created based on information and reasoning.

The second knowledge process is knowledge sharing, which involves the dissemination of knowledge to benefit others. For example, the sales VP sends his findings by e-mail to the executive team so that they can learn the latest thinking on product pricing.

The third knowledge process is knowledge use. Companies must use their knowledge in order to get value from it. That is, knowledge must be put to work to generate wealth. Having read the VP's e-mail, the head of product pricing adjusts pricing for key products and therefore improves sales performance.

The first knowledge enabler is vision and strategy. A cross-functional organization's strategy should encourage knowledge management to promote the creation, sharing, and use of knowledge. For example, the CEO of an IT company mandates that 20% of the features of a new product should come from the company's knowledge base.

The second knowledge enabler is roles and skills. A cross-functional organization should define dedicated roles to help create, share, and use knowledge. For example, the CEO of the IT company appoints a VP whose task is to implement knowledge management systems in the organization.

Policies, processes, tools, and platforms should be put in place to standardize and streamline knowledge dissemination and uptake. For example, the VP responsible for knowledge management puts in place a company-wide knowledge management system. The VP also ensures that the system is supported by the appropriate policies and processes.

The value of knowledge management

Knowledge management is a valuable tool in furthering cross-functional strategies. When implemented in cross-functional organizations, knowledge management systems can improve performance in terms of cost, time, and quality.

Knowledge management can further cross-functionality in five ways:
- it helps to overcome organizational silos
- it enables people to work across functions
- it fosters solutions that benefit the entire organization
- it supports knowledge sharing, learning, and expertise, and
- it encourages unity around common goals in the organization

Organizational silos occur when functional units work in isolation without considering the effect their actions have on the rest of the organization.

The first way that knowledge management furthers cross-functionality is that it overcomes organizational silos. It does this by aligning all systems to enable the free flow of information up, down, and between functions.

Consider this example. A knowledge management database is implemented at an Internet service provider to allow everyone in the company to record customer meetings, customer support issues, and customer requirements. Within six months, all departments have a complete picture of customer issues and needs.

The second way that knowledge management fosters cross-functionality is by enabling people to work across functions by providing information in a collective setting. This is a setting where people can communicate the status of work items, identify patterns in data, and share lessons learned.

Communicate status

Knowledge management enables the status of work items to be shared between departments. For example, at the Internet service provider, the entire organization can see the status of a fix for a customer problem as it's handed over from engineering to testing, and finally to release. The company benefits because everyone can see how problems get resolved.

Identify patterns in data

Knowledge management enables people to spot patterns in data to help them predict future trends. For example, at the Internet service provider, the Marketing Department can see from customer usage data that sales have decreased 10% per quarter for the past three quarters. The company benefits by fixing problems before they become issues.

Share lessons learned

Sharing lessons learned enables organizations to learn from past mistakes and adopt best practices. For example, at the Internet service provider, the sales team gains insights about customer needs from reading the marketing team's frequently asked questions on the company web site. The company benefits by increasing employee knowledge.

The third way that knowledge management supports cross-functionality is that it fosters solutions that benefit the entire organization. Knowledge management helps people share the information needed to develop a complete understanding of the organization and its goals.

It can supply on-demand information that can be shared across boundaries. This enables the organization to deal with and remedy problems.

The Marketing and Planning Departments of the Internet service provider use a database to record and understand customers' web browsing needs. The company's mission statement is then updated accordingly. The company benefits by having the entire organization aligned with the new mission statement.

The fourth way that knowledge management furthers cross-functionality is that it supports the sharing of knowledge and expertise. By doing this, it enables collaboration across functions and locations.

Data about the organization, its market, its customers, and its competition needs to be dispersed to create value. Most important are the patterns in this data, which need to be revealed so that accurate predictions can be made.

The Operations Department at the Internet service provider has created an analysis of customer usage and stored it on the knowledge management system. The Marketing Department further analyzes the data to plan advertising campaigns, the Sales Department uses it to amend pricing, and the Engineering Department uses it to help plan network expansions.

The fifth way that knowledge management fosters cross-functionality is by encouraging the organization to unify around common goals.

Knowledge management helps drive a single objective across the organization. This avoids the pitfall of having people in each function placing focus on that function and losing sight of the overall objective. With a knowledge management system, people can make strategic decisions with the overall objective in mind.

The CEO at the Internet service provider formulates a new goal to expand into new geographic regions. The company knowledge management system is used to spread the message of the new goal and drive the company objective. Within six months, the company has expanded into two new regions.

Knowledge management approaches

You've learned about the value of knowledge management in furthering an organization's cross- functional strategies. There are some specific knowledge management approaches that you can use to facilitate the flow of experience and skills in your organization.

Four knowledge management approaches in particular have been found to work well. These are communities of practice, knowledge repositories, action reviews, and best practice replication. All of these are approaches that can enhance organizational cross-functionality.

Communities of practice

Communities of practice are groups of people with a common interest. They work together to learn, solve problems, and develop new ideas.

Knowledge repositories

Knowledge repositories are computer systems that allow users to capture and organize the knowledge assets of an organization. This enables rapid searching, viewing, and retrieval of knowledge.

Action reviews

Action reviews are facilitated reviews conducted before, during, or after work activities. During these reviews, project members jointly analyze lessons learned with a view to future improvements.

Best practice replication

Best practice replication is a structured process to collect and publish innovative practices or solutions. These can then be adopted by the rest of the organization.

Cultivating communities of practice in your organization is one knowledge management strategy. Communities of practice are groups whose members regularly share knowledge and learn from each other. People who collaborate in communities of practice display some distinctive characteristics. They share common work activities or interests. They recognize the collective value of sharing knowledge. Finally, they have developed norms of trust, reciprocity, and cooperation.

As a leader, you should encourage your teams to collaborate across functions. Communities of practice are the ideal environment for experts across departments to exchange ideas with their peers. This is the most powerful way to convey knowledge between individuals of an organization. For example, a newspaper editor sets up a web community of IT and communications professionals to share ideas on how the Internet can be used as a publishing tool.

The second knowledge management approach is to use knowledge repositories. These organize and store the sum total of an organization's expertise and experience. A repository is computer based and allows access to a number of knowledge sources in a variety of representations. It enables people to query, manage, and integrate results from available knowledge sources.

Knowledge repositories may contain such useful knowledge as lessons learned, best practices, and planning documents. They can be used by the entire organization to improve processes.

Knowledge can be stored as text or hypertext. It can also be stored as images, video, or audio. Knowledge can be organized in different ways – for example by topic or by document type.

For example, a cell phone operator sets up a database to record details of customer preferences for cell phones. On the other hand, the Sales Department uses images of cell phones stored in the database to target sales of new phones to customers.

Using action reviews is a third knowledge management approach. Action reviews identify and capture lessons at project milestones or on completion of a project. Typically the questions addressed include, "Did this project achieve what it was supposed to?" "What was actually achieved?" and, most crucial, "What should be done differently in the future?" Action reviews are used as inputs to future planning so that others can avoid similar issues.

Action reviews are a way for teams to examine and record what they did during the course of a project. In a cross-functional organization, these reviews speed up competence improvements. They can also help teams to focus on goals by reviewing their success in meeting deadlines.

For example, when a project concludes, the project manager invites all project participants to an action review to examine what went right and what went wrong. The engineering team leader notes that some work items were dropped in the handoff from engineering to testing. The project manager notes the issue in the knowledge base and makes a minor adjustment to the testing process so that the problem will not reoccur.

Best practice replication is the fourth knowledge management approach. It is based on the idea that no situation is entirely unique – someone in the organization has solved the problem or overcome the difficulty before. Likewise, people who have "been there before" want to share what they know with others. Best practice replication brings the knowledge and the need together by collating and publishing best practices for use in the rest of the organization.

Ford Motor Company developed and formalized best practice replication in the 1990s when executives realized the need to drive manufacturing globally, rather than regionally. Executives recognized that regional, cultural, and process differences existed, but there was no obvious way to pick out the best process or manufacturing method.

The challenge for the company was to find a way for operations in remote locations to learn from each other without the need to travel.

The solution was to use Ford's intranet to collate, document, and share key best practices from manufacturing plants globally. This allowed engineers to learn about and adopt the best manufacturing practices.

Learning Aid - **The Four Knowledge Management Approaches**

Knowledge management is a valuable tool in furthering an organization's cross-functional strategies. The combination of knowledge management and cross-functional structures improves organizational performance in terms of cost, time, and quality.

Knowledge management approach	Description
Communities of practice	Communities of practice are groups whose members regularly share knowledge and learn from each other. They work together to learn, solve problems, or develop new ideas.
Knowledge repositories	Knowledge repositories are computer systems that capture, analyze, and organize the knowledge assets of an organization to enable easy searching, viewing, and retrieval.
Action reviews	Action reviews are facilitated reviews conducted before, during, or after important work activities. During these reviews, project members jointly analyze lessons learned.
Best practice replication	Best practice replication is a structured process to collect and publish innovative practices or solutions. These can then be adopted by the rest of the organization.

Learning Aid - Implementing the Four Knowledge Management Approaches

You can use this document to record how the four knowledge management approaches could be implemented in your organization.

Knowledge management approach	Description
Communities of practice	
Knowledge repositories	
Action reviews	
Best practice replication	

Learning Aid - The Four Principles to Support Strategic Cross-functionality

To survive and compete, many organizations are developing cross-functional structures. They recognize how the strengths and flexibility of this new structure can help them respond to business challenges.

Principal to support strategic cross-functionality	Example
Blend top-down and bottom-up orientations	The executive team at a legal firm outlines a vision for how the company will expand over the next three years. However, middle managers and senior lawyers define the steps to achieve the vision.
Develop a cross-functional culture	The CEO of an Internet service provider wants to make rapid product delivery one of the company's core values. The CEO visits each company site to get the message across to everyone in the company.
Define goals clearly	The executive team at an aircraft manufacturer defines the company's top level goal as "always meeting customer expectations for time and quality deliveries."
Communicate appropriately	The executive team of a bank promotes its new cross-functional management structure by presenting the new organization chart and management processes to staff at each branch of the bank.

Learning Aid - Knowledge Categories, Processes, and Enablers

Knowledge management works with different

- categories of organizational knowledge, including tacit knowledge, explicit knowledge, and cultural knowledge
- knowledge processes, including knowledge creation, knowledge sharing, and knowledge use
- knowledge enablers, including vision and strategy; roles and skills; policies, processes, tools and platforms

Knowledge categories

Knowledge category	Description
Tacit knowledge	Knowledge that's difficult to transfer to another person by means of writing it down or verbalizing it. For example, the ability to use a programming language to create a new web browser. This would require knowledge that's not always known explicitly.
Explicit knowledge	Knowledge that can be easily recorded, transmitted, and understood by a recipient. For example, the fact that the head of a company is called a CEO.
Cultural knowledge	Knowledge gained from experience. For example, a salesperson's knowledge of customers' buying habits and preferences.

Knowledge processes

Knowledge process	Description
Knowledge creation	The creation of facts or skills acquired through experience or learning. For example, a sales manager creates a sales spreadsheet. The sales VP then notes on the spreadsheet that some products have reduced sales – this is information. The VP then uses competitor information and judgment to conclude that some products are overpriced. In this case, knowledge has been created based on information and reasoning.
Knowledge sharing	Involves the dissemination of knowledge so that others can benefit from it. For example, the sales VP sends his findings by e-mail along with the spreadsheet to the executive team so that they can learn the latest thinking on product pricing.
Knowledge use	Must happen to get value from knowledge and generate knowledge capital. For example, having read the VP's e-mail, the head of product pricing adjusts pricing for key products, and so improves sales performance.

Knowledge enablers

Knowledge enabler	Description
Vision and strategy	An organization's vision and strategy should encourage knowledge management to promote the creation, sharing, and use of knowledge. For example, the CEO of an IT company mandates that 20% of the features of a new product should come from the company's knowledge base.
Roles and skills	A cross-functional organization should recognize the contribution of knowledge management by defining dedicated knowledge management roles and skills. For example, the CEO of the IT company appoints a VP whose task is to implement knowledge management systems in the organization.
Policies, processes,	Policies, processes, tools, and platforms should be put in place to standardize and streamline knowledge dissemination and uptake within the organization.

CHAPTER THREE

Managing for Rapid Change and Uncertainty

Managing for Rapid Change and Uncertainty

Although there are many reasons why organizational change might be necessary, every major transformation has an impact on employees. Unless it's properly managed, organizational change can result in increased absenteeism, reduced productivity, and the loss of valued employees.

There are five guiding principles for effective change management: address the "people issues," involve every level of the organization, create ownership, communicate the message, and take account of the culture.

Leadership during change requires preparation, which involves a number of steps. First, identify the changes that affect your group. Second, adapt to these changes, which includes communicating any concerns. Finally, acquire the skills to manage the change, which means grasping the principles of change management, mastering the tools of change management, and formulating action plans.

It's also necessary to prepare the organization for change. There are five steps to doing this: determine what needs to change, create the need for change, ensure strong support from upper management, develop a strategy and specific plans, and manage the doubts and concerns of all those involved.

Once implemented, changes need to be reinforced and embedded within the organization. There are four measures a manager can use to do this.

First, the changes must be woven into the organization's culture, which requires you to identify barriers and supports to the changes. Second, it's necessary to sustain the changes, which is done by getting the support of the leadership, adapting the structure of the organization, and implementing a system of accountability. Third, it's necessary to evaluate the change process. You do this by checking for success, collecting data, analyzing employee feedback, and conducting a root cause analysis.

Finally, it's important to celebrate successes, which means recognizing and rewarding achievements.

Nature of organizational change

Like it or not, every major organization needs to maintain a constant focus on change. The days when organizations could count on stability are gone. In an era of market transparency, labor mobility, and globalization, change is inevitable – and almost the only thing that organizations can be sure of.

Organizational change is the process of transformation that an organization undergoes when adapting to something new. This could be due to a change in strategy, management, goals, or objectives – which could come about as a result of a merger, an acquisition, or general restructuring. During this process of transformation, management must address several challenges by adopting best practice standards.

When the organization's units are closely integrated, these challenges are especially difficult.

This is because a change in one unit can have a profound ripple effect throughout the entire organization.

For example, a cut in annual budget allocated to an organization's Marketing Department will likely impact its Sales Department and Production Department as well.

You may have thought of things like mergers, acquisitions, or the introduction of new technology as being among the developments that could create a need for organizational change. There's actually no end to the number of things that might lead to organizational change. Other common examples are restructuring or downsizing, legislative or regulatory changes, changes in customers' needs, cuts in funding or a redirection of resources, or entry into a new market or exit from an old one.

Although there are a wide range of potential causes of organizational change, there's one constant – its impact on employees. The main challenge this poses for management is in dealing with the uncertainty that's inevitably caused. It can affect employees psychologically, emotionally, and physically.

Many people function within a comfort zone, and they often put up barriers to protect these zones. Some are deeply attached to the way they work, and tend to want to keep things as they are.

Change can threaten this comfort zone. It can challenge a person's values and central core beliefs, causing stress. Not knowing what's coming down the line may create confusion, anxiety, and uncertainty.

Generally, change may be resisted if it requires people to step outside their comfort zones. When
confused and anxious, people may withdraw, become skeptical and distrustful, and prioritize self-protection and survival over everything else.

One reason for resistance to change is that people often personalize the need for change. When they're told that the current way of doing something is going to change, what they hear is "you're not valued."

A negative response to change almost always stems from leadership's failure to communicate what lies ahead. People wouldn't be as resistant to change if they understood the meaning and relevance of the change.

This is why it's so important to manage and lead change. Doing this effectively requires an understanding of the human factors involved.

Benefits of managing change

Poorly managed organizational change can affect employees on psychological, emotional, and physical levels. This can lead to workdays missed through illness as worried employees work longer hours to protect their positions, which causes stress and damage to their health. Employees are also less productive due to the deterioration in working relationships as competition intensifies. And valued employees – those with confidence, skill, and experience – may leave in response to the level of uncertainty surrounding them.

However, effective management of the change can help eliminate the negative effects, reduce the level of uncertainty within the organization, and accelerate the change process, with goals achieved more quickly. Poor management has the opposite effect.

For example, consider the case of Susan, the managing director of a multinational company with an extensive portfolio of branded products. One of the company's most famous products is nearing the end of its product life cycle. Although many have a sentimental attachment to the product, its sales are poor and it has in many ways been superseded by technological developments.

As well as scaling back production, Susan decides to reallocate the product's annual development budget. She decides that its development and marketing teams – including the managers who oversee these functions – will be assigned to other divisions within the company that have products and brands with strong growth potential.

Susan wants to implement these changes immediately, so she looks to avoid any protracted discussion. She e-mails the managers with details of the change and the new role being assigned to each. Although Susan knows this will be an unpleasant surprise to many – some of the managers have worked with this brand for over a decade – she's convinced there's no alternative.

In the first month after announcing the change, Susan is disappointed with the response. Some managers have told her the decision is ill-judged and unfair. Others, she feels, are clearly resisting the change – they're only half-heartedly performing their new roles. There's also been a noticeable decline in morale.

She's also disappointed that three managers – who she had high hopes for in their new roles – have resigned. She's heard rumors that others are actively seeking alternative employment. She wonders if this is the reason for the spike in absenteeism.

The reorganization itself also isn't going as smoothly as hoped. There's been no improvement in productivity from the divisions that have been given the additional resources.

Principles of change management

Organizational change is a systematic approach to addressing change. It involves the application of knowledge and resources to addressing this change. There are three principal activities involved in effective change management. First, it's about defining and implanting new values and behaviors that support a new approach to how things are done. Second, it's about building consensus around changes that will benefit all involved. Third, it's about planning, testing, and implementing every aspect of the change.

There are several guiding principles of change management. It's important to address the "people issues" of a transformation. It's also important to involve every level of the organization, and instill a sense of responsibility for making change happen – which means creating ownership. To ensure that everyone understands the new direction, it's important to communicate the message. Finally, it's vital to take account of the culture of the organization.

Address the "people issues"

Effective management of change requires you to address the "people issues" that inevitably result from major transformations.

A major transformation makes significant demands on people, such as changing their jobs or asking them to learn new skills. This causes uncertainty, which can lead to resistance.

Morale and results will suffer unless there's a formal arrangement in place, developed early and adjusted as necessary.

Involve every level of the organization

It's important to involve every level of the organization simply because a transformation – from its design to its implementation – affects every level.

Within the overall plan for organizational change, it's a good idea to identify leaders throughout the organization, at every level, and make them responsible for the implementation. Doing this ensures that change flows through the organization, from level to level.

Create ownership

There needs to be more than just passive acceptance of the change process – there needs to be a sense of ownership among a sufficient number of individuals. These are leaders who are prepared to take responsibility for implementing the change wherever they have influence or control.

Communicate the message

Instead of assuming that others understand the issues or the reasons for the change, communicate the message. Do this in an inspirational and practicable way. Communication should be regular and timely, and done through several different channels.

Take account of the culture

When devising the new approach to doing things, take account of the culture and behaviors within the organization. Early assessment of the organization's culture will help you identify potential difficulties and conflicts before they emerge, and also determine the readiness to change. Any change has to take account of – and be consistent with – the core values, beliefs, and behaviors of the organization.

Leading organizational change

As a manager, you have a vital role to play in implementing change. You're on the front line when new processes, systems, or job roles take effect. You also play a critical leadership role during times of change and uncertainty. You need to be a communicator, an advocate of change, a facilitator of learning, a point of contact, and a process owner.

Communicator

Being a communicator is a fundamental requirement of managers when driving organizational change. It's about having open, frank discussions with direct reports.

To drive change, managers must be central to the delivery of information – that is, information must be channeled through them. An otherwise effective communications campaign will fail without this kind of direct interaction.

Advocate of change

Managers need to be advocates of change, which entails a personal commitment to support and participate in the change process. This means identifying the specific changes that will affect your direct reports, understanding the reasons for these changes, knowing how your team will be affected, and understanding your role in the process.

Introducing the change to your group includes building an awareness of the need for the change and the objectives of the change. It's your job to promote the change to your team.

Facilitator of learning

During organizational change, managers are facilitators of learning. This requires regular, on-the-job training in the new processes.

Intensive training given by specialized trainers is useful, but it can't replace hands-on, on-the-job training by managers.

Point of contact

Managers serve as points of contact between those involved in the change process, acting as liaisons between different groups.

Just as information should be channeled through managers, feedback should be solicited and channeled back up through the line of communication.

Regular meetings between managers and direct reports are an opportunity to identify problems and brainstorm ideas for improvement.

Process owner

It's not enough to have a high-level understanding of the change process. You need to be a process owner.

Taking ownership of the process means understanding it and being an expert in its details. It means knowing about the changes and how they connect with and impact upon other functions, and understanding your role in the change process.

It also means being a change champion – encouraging buy-in from others, and taking responsibility for making change happen.

Leading change requires preparation. You prepare to be a leader during change by identifying the changes that will affect your group, adapting to these changes, and acquiring the skills to manage the change process.

The first step in preparing to lead change is to identify the changes that affect your group. Not every change will impact upon your direct reports, while others may severely affect them. You must determine the specific impact of changes on your team. It's also important to know why the changes are necessary, and to understand your own role in the process.

Determining the specific impact of changes is about identifying the implications for your team. What specific things will they have to do differently?

Consider, for example, a consumer goods company that's undergoing a transformation to make its new product development more innovative and responsive to consumer needs.

For the Product Development Department, this change requires a dramatic shift in thinking and approach. However, for the Accounting Department, the impact of the change is minor.

It's also important to know why the changes are necessary. In the previous example, it could be that the company is being overshadowed by its competitors, who are developing more creative and exciting products. The company's future prospects are poor unless its product offering is improved.

To develop an understanding of your own role in the process, consider what you need to do to drive the change process. This means assessing your responsibilities and how these are affected by the changes.

For example, for the human resources manager in the consumer goods company, the recruitment policy may need to change to prioritize the recruitment of creative individuals. His role would be to recruit such people, and also to develop the capabilities of existing employees who have creative talents.

The second step in preparing to lead change is to adapt to the changes. This involves reflecting on your own resistance, if any, to the changes, and communicating your concerns.

It's important to reflect on your own resistance. There could be aspects of how your department functions that you're attached to – either sentimentally or professionally. For example, perhaps the change plan involves terminating a program that you initiated. Although you may not like this, be honest with yourself about the true motivations behind your resistance.

Communicating your concerns is also an important part of adapting to the changes. Perhaps you doubt your department's ability to meet a particular requirement of the change plan. This information should be communicated to whoever is overseeing the change process.

The second step in preparing to lead change is to adapt to the changes. This involves reflecting on your own resistance, if any, to the changes, and communicating your concerns.

It's important to reflect on your own resistance. There could be aspects of how your department functions that you're attached to – either sentimentally or professionally. For example, perhaps the change plan involves terminating a program that you initiated. Although you may not like this, be honest with yourself about the true motivations behind your resistance.

Communicating your concerns is also an important part of adapting to the changes. Perhaps you doubt your department's ability to meet a particular requirement of the change plan. This information should be communicated to whoever is overseeing the change process.

Stakeholder mapping

You use stakeholder mapping to identify the key stakeholders – those with the power to either obstruct or drive the change process – and involve them early in the process. It's also a good idea to devise a specific plan for how you'll engage them so that they can contribute to the project.

For example, you might identify middle managers as being the key stakeholders because of the influence they have over employees. Their cooperation and endorsement would be critical. Because of this, it would be prudent to engage with them and involve them early in the process.

Culture mapping

Using the culture mapping tool means considering the culture of the organization – the assumptions, values, and behaviors – when preparing for change. The culture might be a source of resistance to the change, and this may have to be tackled before the change is implemented.

For example, one aspect of the change plan might be to promote individuals based on merit in an effort to improve the caliber of senior management. However, the culture could be for individuals to progress in accordance with seniority.

Force field analysis

The force field analysis tool gives you an overview of the drivers for change and the inhibitors of change.

When preparing the organization for change, you would consider what factors will aid the change, and how you can reinforce them. You would also consider the factors that might obstruct the change and how you can reduce these obstructions. This gives you an insight into what you can do to drive the change.

For example, the main inhibitor to change may be familiarity and comfort with the current system. You could reduce this obstruction by emphasizing the benefits of the new system.

Acquiring change management skills also means formulating action plans that guide others through the change process. An action plan should explain the implementation and measurement of the changes. People should know what the interim goals are and what metrics will be used to assess progress. It's also necessary to ensure clarity on individual roles and responsibilities. People should understand their individual roles in the change process. They should know what they're accountable for, and who they're accountable to.

Preparing an organization for change

Effective organizational change requires preparation. The organization must recognize the need for change and be capable of changing. Only then can the existing system be dismantled and a new way of operating created.

There are five steps to preparing an organization for change: determine what needs to change, create the need for change, ensure strong support from upper management, develop a strategy and specific plans, and manage doubts and concerns.

Determine what needs to change

The first step is to determine what needs to change. Change won't happen until there's strong motivation to change.

This begins with an assessment of the organization's current state and a rethinking of the ingrained assumptions that the organization has. This fosters understanding of why change is necessary.

Create the need for change

Creating the need for change begins with a compelling communication about why the change is necessary. This means showing why the current approach or system is inappropriate.

Convincing others of the need for change can be done through quantifiable metrics – for example, falling sales, poor financial results, or unflattering customer satisfaction survey results. This information strengthens the case for change.

You should also present your own vision and strategy as supporting evidence. This vision should be communicated in terms of the change required, with an emphasis on why the change is necessary.

Ensure strong support

Preparing an organization for change requires you to ensure strong support from upper management. This means identifying the key stakeholders within the organization, and winning their support for the change process.

Changing the way an organization functions often provokes resistance. However, using stakeholder analysis and stakeholder management, this resistance can be overcome by helping people recognize the benefits that change will bring.

The need for change should be presented as an issue of organization-wide importance.

Develop a strategy and specific plans

Developing a strategy and specific plans is an important component in preparing an organization for change. It's a good idea to put in place a Change Advisory Board – a group of individuals drawn from every area that the change affects. This allows all stakeholders to have an opportunity to contribute and safeguard their interests.

The Change Advisory Board should meet regularly to discuss the change plan. A schedule should be created so everyone is aware of what's happening. It's also necessary to ensure that there aren't any overlaps with other important procedures.

Manage doubts and concerns

When preparing an organization for change, it's necessary to manage the doubts and concerns of all those affected. This means remaining open to and addressing others' concerns.

It's inevitable that some people will lose out during change – especially those who benefit from the current system. Others may find it difficult to see the benefits of change. People need time and information to understand why the changes are being introduced. They also need to feel involved in the transition process.

Consider the example of Louis, the human resources manager of a telecommunications company. Consumer research findings show that the decline in the company's market share is due to the poor level of customer service provided by the company. The company is positioned as a low-price, no-frills service provider, but the research also shows that this no longer appeals to consumers.

The board of directors meets to determine what needs to change, and decides to dramatically improve the company's customer service. Louis has been asked to oversee the change process.

Louis aims first to create the need for change. In consultation with the board – and particularly with those directors responsible for customer service, marketing, and customer accounts – he compiles a plan for the transformation. This includes the data on the company's declining market share and the findings of the recent consumer research.

This information is especially useful in ensuring strong support from the marketing director. Initially, she was reluctant to abandon her three-year marketing plan. However, she now accepts the need for all future marketing initiatives to promote the company as one that cares about its customers.

Louis next develops a strategy and specific plans. He creates a Change Advisory Board, involving himself, the marketing manager, the customer support manager, and the customer accounts manager. The idea is to meet on a weekly basis to review progress.

These meetings also offer an opportunity to manage doubts and concerns. For example, in response to the customer support manager's concern, additional resources are allocated to that department so it can cope with the extra demand. This allows customer call center operatives to spend more time on calls from customers and for the customer complaints division to respond more thoroughly.

Guidelines for implementation

The implementation of change is a distinct stage in overall organizational change. It's appropriate only when the organization has prepared for change, when the early uncertainty has abated and people are open to a new way of acting. This is the time to implement or introduce the change. When implementing a change plan, there are three tasks: secure commitment, dispel rumors, and involve people.

The first task when implementing change is to secure commitment from those involved. You do this by communicating the nature of the change and why it's necessary, describing the effects of the change on everyone, and clarifying the aims and benefits of the change.

Communicate nature of change

Securing commitment begins with communicating the nature of the change and why the change is necessary.

Employees need to know the reasons for the change, the origins of the need, and the risks of not implementing the change.

It's natural for people to resist change at first. Explaining the nature of the change and why it's necessary will aid acceptance.

Describe effects of change

Clearly describing the effects of the change is an important part of securing commitment. People need to know how the change will affect them, and how their roles will change.

If employees are uncertain about the change's impact, insecurity and uncertainty will grow, affecting morale and causing resistance.

Clarify aims and benefits

Securing commitment requires clarity about the aims of the change and emphasis on the benefits. This means first being clear about what the change is intended to achieve and why it's important that the organization achieves this aim.

When confronted with change, employees will often ask "what's in it for me?" The benefit could be a financial bonus or a promotion. Or it could be action on an unsatisfactory aspect of the current system, a greater sense of belonging, or more trust and respect. Often, the benefit will involve job security.

Increasing awareness of the aims and benefits of the change will make employees more motivated to make the change happen.

Consider John, the production manager at a manufacturing company. When implementing change, John explains the nature of the change and the reasons for it. In this case, to meet the aggressive production targets set by senior management, he needs to introduce new machinery.

He also explains the effects of the change on individuals. He tells employees that although there will be no job losses, training will be needed.

John is also clear about the aims of the change, and he emphasizes the benefits. He tells employees that the aims are to increase output and efficiency. He explains that this will lead to greater profitability, which will be reflected in pay.

Follow along as John and Becky, a line manager, discuss the change.

Becky: So what's this big change everyone's talking about? Why now? I thought things were fine.

Becky is skeptical.

John: They are. Management wants us to scale up production, to be a far bigger operation. But to do that, we need better, more modern machinery and equipment.

John is positive and encouraging.

Becky: Looks like things are going to be very different around here...well, different for some.

Becky is skeptical and suspicious.

John: Yes, to an extent. And the new machinery is more complicated than what we've been using. People will need training. But everything else will be the same.

John is honest and genuine.

Becky: Everything except for the hours we'll be working. It'll take time to adjust. I bet there'll be some long days ahead.

Becky is cynical.

John: No, Becky. I know it'll be a challenge, but everyone will be supported. Plus, I've been assured that efficiency savings and increased profits will be shared. We'll all benefit.

John is confident and assuring.

Becky: Well, when you put it like that, I guess it sounds like a good idea.

Becky is positive and thoughtful. Becky is agreeable.

John: It's exactly like I said. The company is in a great position for growth, but we need to increase our production capacity in order to capitalize on this opportunity.

John is firm and reassuring.

John effectively dispels the rumor that's circulating. He answers Becky's question directly and honestly. When told of the rumor, he commits to addressing the problem immediately. And he reassures Becky about the reasons behind the change by referring back to the operational necessities.

The third task when implementing change is to involve people. You can do this by facilitating employee involvement, developing individual action plans, and reinforcing the change by generating short-term success.

It's important to facilitate employee involvement so employees feel like they're part of what's happening. You can involve employees by listening to their opinions, suggestions, and criticisms, and by giving them input into the details of the change. For example, recognizing that it's the employees who will be working with the new machinery, John asks for their views on the equipment.

It's also necessary to develop individual action plans to enable individuals to implement and adjust to the change. Employees may need assistance in adapting to new roles or responsibilities. For example, aware that his employees lack the technical knowledge to operate the new machinery, John organizes training tailored to their individual needs.

A manager should also reinforce the change through the generation of short-term successes. This means celebrating interim achievements, which enables earlier identification of success. This reinforces employees' efforts to keep working toward the goals. For example, John is targeting a 30% increase in output in the first quarter. When the first month's figures show the company is on course, he announces it with excitement.

Actions that reinforce change

Any changes that have been implemented within an organization need to be internalized so that they become part of its daily functioning. This means reinforcing and embedding the changes into the organization. A manager does this by weaving the changes into the culture, sustaining the changes, evaluating the process, and celebrating success.

Having implemented the changes, try to weave them into the organization's culture. This ensures that employees continue to behave in a way that meets the objectives the changes were intended to achieve. Even if the changes were embraced initially, people may revert to the old way of doing things if the changes weren't properly ingrained into the culture.

It's necessary to first identify barriers to sustaining the changes. Some employees revert to the old way out of familiarity. Or they may feel ill-equipped to act in the new way. This often happens when management doesn't allocate enough resources to enable real adoption of the changes. It's necessary to provide training that offers genuine hands-on experience with the new procedures.

Then identify what supports the changes. It's important that the culture be conducive to the changes, which means proper training and preparation. Changes can also be supported through financial and nonfinancial incentives, which can help maintain people's motivation.

Another way a manager can reinforce and embed implemented changes is by developing measures to sustain the changes. Ways of sustaining changes include getting the support of the leadership of the organization, adapting the structure of the organization, and implementing a system of accountability.

Get support from leadership

If a change program is to be sustained, it's essential to get leadership support.

Employees infer what's important from the behavior of management – and actions count more than words.

Adapt structure of the organization

Sustaining the change effort entails adapting the structure of the organization. A new structure that reinforces the new way of doing things must be developed. This also means developing rules, policies, customs, and behaviors that reinforce the new approach.

Implement system of accountability

It's also necessary to implement a system of accountability. If the change is to be sustained, it must be continually managed and measured with a clear understanding of who's accountable for what.

It's a good idea to establish a feedback mechanism that gives a clear picture of progress and performance so that people don't feel their efforts are wasted. This also provides an incentive to work toward the objectives of the change, as it makes it clear who's accountable for each component.

The third way a manager can reinforce and embed implemented changes is by evaluating the process. Ways of evaluating the process include checking for success through a post-implementation review, collecting data on the change process, analyzing employee feedback, and conducting a root cause analysis.

It's important to check for success to ensure that the objectives have been achieved. A post- implementation review should set out to answer three fundamental questions about the change process: did it resolve the issues it was intended to address? Is there scope for improvements that could deliver even greater benefits? Are there lessons to be learned that could be applied to future initiatives?

Evaluating the process also entails collecting data that enables a performance assessment of the change process. This helps management to determine whether the change has had the intended impact and to identify problems.

It's also necessary to solicit and analyze employee feedback. You do this to assess how employees are reacting to the changes. This will highlight any difficulties that are being encountered and identify potential improvements.

It's also important to conduct a root cause analysis if there are post-implementation problems. This will indicate the corrective action required.

The final way a manager can reinforce and embed implemented changes is by celebrating success. Ways of celebrating success include recognizing success and achievements, and then rewarding these achievements. The recognition of success should be immediate, personal, and sincere. Recognizing and rewarding success helps employees find closure on the period of transformation. It also shows appreciation for their efforts during a difficult time and gives them confidence that future changes will be successful.

Learning Aid - The Principles of Change Management

There are a number of guiding principles for transformational change to consider when managing a change process.

Guideline	Explanation
Deal with the "people issues"	As part of effective change management, the "people issues" that inevitably result from major transformations need to be addressed. This means addressing the uncertainty and anxiety that result from changing roles or requiring new skills to be learned.
Involve every level of the organization	Because a major transformation affects every level of the organization, it's important to involve every level affected by the change plan. A good approach is to identify leaders throughout the organization, at every level, and make them responsible for the implementation.
Create ownership	There needs to be a sense of ownership among a core of individuals at every level of the organization. These are leaders who take responsibility for implementing the change wherever they have influence.
Communicate the message	The issues or the reasons for the change must be communicated in an inspirational and practicable way, ideally through several different channels.
Take account of the culture	When devising the new approach to doing things that underpins the transformation, it's important to take account of the culture of the organization. Change must take account of – and be consistent with – the core values, beliefs, and behaviors of the organization.

Learning Aid - Applying the principles in preparing for change

You can print this document or recreate the table in a word processing or spreadsheet application and use it to complete this activity.

Consider a change process that is underway or imminent in your organization. Using the table provided, assess how you have prepared or are preparing for this change.

Principle	Specific requirements	Your action
Identify changes that affect your group	Determine the specific impact Understand the reasons for the change Understand your own role in the process	
Adapt to these changes	Communicate your concerns Reflect on your own resistance	
Acquire the skills to manage change	Grasp the principles of change management Master the tools of change management Formulate action plans	

Learning Aid - Principles for Reinforcing Organizational Change

Principle	Application
Weave changes into culture	This is about anchoring the change within the organization's culture. It's done by identifying both supports and barriers to sustaining the change.
Sustain the changes	It's necessary to create an environment that sustains the change. This is done by ensuring senior management supports the change, adapting the structure of the organization, and implementing a system of accountability.
Evaluate the process	Evaluating the process gives an indication of how successful the change process has been. This can be done by checking for success through a post-implementation review, collecting data on the change process, analyzing employee feedback, and conducting a root cause analysis.
Celebrate success	It's important to celebrate successes and achievements associated with the change process. Do this by recognizing success and achievements, and then rewarding these achievements.

CHAPTER FOUR

Managing High Performers

Managing High Performers

By managing your high performers carefully, you can help them exceed expectations and add value to your organization.

High performers share a number of characteristics. They tend to view work as more than a job – it's something they're passionate about. In most cases, they know exactly what they're good at and choose careers that exploit their strengths. They usually have clear goals in life and high expectations of themselves and others. They're generally enthusiastic about their work. They also look for challenges in their work and like to have autonomy over it.

Managers should do all they can to retain high performers. High performers raise the general performance of their organizations. Retaining them avoids the cost of hiring and training replacement employees. It avoids the loss of morale among coworkers. And it preserves the company's reputation, client relationships, and intellectual capital.

There are five techniques you can use to develop the potential of your high performers and keep them motivated.

First, you should ensure you reward high performers fairly. It's also important to provide them with meaningful and challenging work. You should allow your high performers to have input into how their work gets done. Ensure the roles you assign them emphasize their strengths. And finally, you can use mentoring to keep them motivated.

Providing motivating feedback can help you retain the high performers in your organization. To provide motivating feedback, you should look for ways to build confidence in your high performers. And your feedback should provide them with guidance and freedom, but not detailed steps to follow.

Importance of high performers

As a manager, if you had the opportunity to build a new workforce, would you rehire all the employees you currently have? It's unlikely you'd choose to keep the least effective performers in your organization. You're more likely to choose individuals who are high performers, or who have the potential to perform at a high level.

High performers tend to pull more than their weight in most organizations. They can be relied upon to meet goals, execute strategies, and generally do excellent work. In fact, they frequently exceed expectations. High performers can help companies be more profitable and successful. However, often their potential to create more value for businesses remains largely untapped.

High performers typically like to work independently. You may believe that because your high performers are performing well, they require little attention. You might focus on your least effective employees instead.

But the fact is high performers require more attention than other employees. While they don't want to be micromanaged, they do require coaching from their managers. They also need regular encouragement, recognition, and feedback if they're to reach their full potential.

By managing your high performers carefully, you can help them surpass expectations – and add value to your organization.

Characteristics of high performers

In order to retain high performers in your organization and benefit from the potential they offer, it's important that you understand what motivates them. High performers generally share a number of common characteristics.

You may have noted that high performers tend to view work as more than a job or a way of earning money – it's something they're passionate about. In most cases, they know exactly what they're good at and choose careers where they can use their strengths. High performers usually have clear goals in life and high expectations of themselves and others. They're generally enthusiastic about their work. They also look for challenges in their work and like to have autonomy over it.

High performers in any profession, from entry-level administrators to corporate vice presidents, view their work as more than a job.

High performers often view their occupations as opportunities to make a difference in the world, to help others, or to prove their own value to the people around them. For example, a high performer working in a technical support role might regard solving a customer's computer problem as a way of improving that person's day and enhancing the company's reputation.

As a result, high performers take their work very seriously and are completely focused on what they're doing. They tend to take on or initiate more projects, work longer hours, and complete significantly more work than their counterparts.

The second characteristic of high performers is that they recognize their own strengths and weaknesses and choose careers where they can use their strengths. For example, a person with superior communication and interpersonal skills could perform brilliantly in customer care or sales. A well-organized person with good planning skills might make an excellent project manager.

The third characteristic of high performers is that they set clear goals for themselves. They focus on results and are often very ambitious. They generally know where they're going in life and have a strategy for getting there.

High performers prefer to follow their own agendas. For example, they may produce exacting schedules for themselves and work to tighter deadlines than you set. Because they're so focused on goals and getting results, they may believe that company rules don't apply to them. They might ignore tried and tested procedures in order to complete tasks more quickly.

The results-driven behavior of high performers can sometimes come across as offensive, disrespectful, or rude. For example, they might read and reply to e-mails during meetings, or act impatiently with teammates who work at a slower pace.

The fourth characteristic of high performers is that they have high expectations of themselves and others. So they frequently make demands on themselves and the people around them.

High performers usually have a "can do" approach, which makes them reluctant to accept that things can't be done. They may well expect others to be as determined as they are to overcome obstacles. For example, high-performing team leaders may state that tight deadlines can be met if the team takes a different approach or works more efficiently. High performers are also ambitious by nature and are more likely to expand on their ideas than scale them back.

High performers are more self-critical and impatient than the average employee. They're also more sensitive to dissatisfaction. What may be a minor irritant to another employee – such as a repetitive assignment or a lack of regular feedback – could be a reason for a high performer to quit.

The fifth characteristic of high performers is that they're enthusiastic about their work. They like to generate joy and meaning from their occupations, and they believe in the wider benefit of what they're doing. High performers typically view work as an opportunity to accomplish things that add value to the lives of others. For example, high-performing salespeople might view the software they're selling as a great way of helping customers be more efficient and have more free time.

The sixth and final characteristic of high performers is that they look for challenges and autonomy. High performers tend to get bored easily, so they need to be challenged at work. So, for example, they like knowing that when one project ends, another challenge lies ahead. And they like to use all their talents to overcome those challenges.

High performers also yearn for responsibility and autonomy over their work. They like to have complete ownership over what they're doing. So when working for others, they often act as if they're operating a business within a business.

They dislike being told what to do and prefer to operate in their own way. They may disregard rules in favor of their own methods. For example, a high-performing salesperson might decide to overlook established guidelines and spend more time in face-to-face meetings with customers in order to increase sales. They thrive in environments that allow them independence and room for innovation.

High performers can be high-maintenance employees, in that they take more effort to manage than other employees.

But high performers are also your greatest asset. By understanding your top performers better and learning to keep them happy, you'll get the most out of them. And your organization will reap the benefits.

Benefits of retaining high performers

High performers are focused and productive individuals. They tend to rise above other employees in terms of value and contribute disproportionately to their organization's success. Retaining top performers can be a continuous struggle. They usually have a higher turnover rate than other employees, as they're always in demand by other employers.

In order to create a retention strategy for high performers, you first need to identify the extent to which high performers are leaving your organization. Then you can look for underlying patterns or reasons why they're leaving and take steps to address those reasons. Even in a tight job market you need a focused retention strategy. High performers are sought-after employees, so not having one could be a costly mistake.

Consider the example of Leroy, who's the top salesperson at the insurance company where he works. Leroy joined the company 18 months ago and rose to the top position in the sales team within six months. He has remained there ever since.

Leroy is clearly a high performer. He attracts more new customers and sells more insurance policies than any other salesperson. He has also repaired several important client relationships that had turned sour by the time he joined the company. The other salespeople are working harder too, in order to keep up with his work rate.

However, without warning, Leroy resigns from the company. He tells his manager, Anna, that the company isn't providing him with a competitive, market-related commission. He also believes he could get more vacation time if he worked elsewhere. Leroy's resignation comes as a shock to Anna, who would like to retain her star performer.

Managers should do all they can to retain employees like Leroy. There are many benefits to be gained by retaining such a high performer:
- the general performance of the company is raised
- the potentially significant costs of hiring and training a replacement are avoided the morale of
- the workforce and important client relationships remain intact, and
- intellectual capital is retained within the organization

Performance of company is raised

High performers usually deliver improved business results for their managers. Their higher-than- average abilities raise the general performance of the organizations they work for. So when high performers leave, there's often a loss of productivity within the organization, which inevitably impacts revenues.

Costs are avoided

Losing high performers can result in high direct costs – in fact, the costs may well exceed the high performers' salaries. It can be expensive to recruit, hire, and train replacement employees.

Morale and relationships remain intact

The loss of a top performer often results in lower morale among the employees who are left behind. Losing a top performer can also jeopardize valued client relationships. Clients may threaten to cancel future orders unless the person who takes over their account delivers the same outstanding level of service as the high performer. It may even diminish the company's reputation among customers and competitors alike.

Intellectual capital is retained

When high performers leave, they often take important intellectual capital with them. This can drain the company's knowledge base, which may take years to recover. Retaining high performers helps to preserve critical information within the company and stops it from walking out the door.

The insurance company where Leroy worked has been negatively affected by his departure. His colleagues have gradually become less productive and their morale has diminished. As a result, the number of new customers they attract has decreased.

The company has to pay the substantial cost of hiring and training a replacement for Leroy. And several existing clients have declined to renew their policies after discovering that Leroy has left.

Leroy has also taken critical knowledge away with him that will take years for the company to restore.

Leroy's manager, Anna, undoubtedly appreciated his excellent output. But she neglected to ensure that her high performer was happy with his rate of commission and vacation benefits. Her neglect has cost her the skill and dedication of a star performer. It's been a costly mistake, but Anna is determined to learn from it. She plans to work harder at retaining the other high performers in the company.

Rewarding high performers

High performers are your organization's best kept secret. They're the most productive and results driven of your employees and can help make your company a success. High performers share a number of characteristics. They tend to view work as more than a job, and choose careers that use their strengths. They have clear goals in life, have high expectations, and are enthusiastic about their work. They also look for challenges and like to have autonomy over their work.

High performers can be difficult to retain because they're always in demand by other employers. As a manager, if you can develop the potential of your high performers and keep them motivated and happy, you have the best chance of retaining them in your organization.

You can use five techniques to motivate and develop the potential of high performers. To begin, you should ensure you reward them fairly. It's also important to provide them with meaningful and challenging work. You should allow your high performers to have input into how their work gets done. Ensure the roles you assign them emphasize their strengths. And finally, you can use mentoring to keep them motivated.

When it comes to rewarding high performers, it's important that they're rewarded and compensated fairly. If competitors are paying much higher salaries for the same work, it could certainly motivate some star performers to leave. But, in general, financial reward isn't the main incentive for them. They may believe other kinds of rewards are more important. Whatever the reward, high performers should be rewarded individually, so their outstanding achievements are acknowledged.

You can reward top talent by offering them flexible and attractive working conditions. For example, a convenient work location, a competitive number of paid vacation days, an adaptable schedule, and flexible working hours can all help you retain your star performers.

Always keep the lines of communication open between you and your top performers. In this way, you'll find out exactly what they want, instead of what you think they want. Then you can do your best to meet their needs and keep them happy.

Consider contacting your high performers on a regular basis and simply asking, "Is there anything I can do for you?" This gesture is sure to be appreciated and should help you discover if they need anything to help them succeed.

Providing challenging work and choice

The second technique you can use to motivate and develop the potential of your high performers is to provide them with meaningful and challenging work. One way of challenging high performers is to give them the opportunity to learn and use new skills. High performers like to feel they're developing and growing. Improving and expanding their skills can help them achieve more, which is a big motivator for them.

Another way of providing meaningful, challenging work is to vary the roles your high performers play. For example, you could rotate their roles, so they're moved between jobs and exposed to all organizational activities. In this way, they'll learn more, they'll be continuously challenged, and they're unlikely to get bored.

Also consider engaging your high performers in the direction of the company. Ensure their goals are aligned to the overall corporate direction. This should motivate them and increase their commitment to the company. For example, if your organization aims to develop an excellent customer support service, put a high performer in charge of limiting customer complaints.

You can also motivate high performers by training them to be experts in their jobs. High performers like to feel they're producing at the highest level possible, so make sure they're well supported. Offer them training whenever possible. Encourage them to attend seminars and conferences, even if it means losing them for a few days.

The third technique for motivating and developing the potential of high performers is to allow them some autonomy over how they get their work done. In other words, while you can tell high performers what to do, don't tell them how to do it. Let them use their own initiative to figure that out.

It makes sense to give your high performers some freedom over how they perform their work. After all, they like to act independently and find innovative ways of doing things. Consider providing them with a forum where they can contribute suggestions about how work is performed in the company. They'll find this highly motivating.

Try to give high performers additional responsibility. They often look for ways to challenge and distinguish themselves in the workplace in order to prove their worth to the company. They may also get bored with a lack of responsibility, which can lead to demotivation.

So delegate tasks to your high performers. Clearly state the results you want to see, set parameters for them, give them whatever support they need, and conduct progress reviews along the way. In such situations, high performers usually rise to the challenge and give their best, and they are likely to excel.

Assigning effective roles and mentoring

The fourth technique you can use to develop the potential of your high performers is to ensure the roles you assign them emphasize their strengths. Employees who regularly use their strengths and talents are more likely to enjoy their work. They're also more likely to work in high-performing teams. Assigning your employees to specific tasks and duties that play to their strengths is one of the best motivation techniques you can use.

When employees are able to use their strengths on a regular basis, they feel effective and fulfilled. They're usually more enthusiastic about their jobs and are inspired to continue doing excellent work. This benefits both the individual and the wider organization.

You can use job sculpting to ensure the tasks you assign to top performers emphasize their strengths. Job sculpting is a technique that matches the interests and aptitudes of high performers to the work they do. It allows high performers to apply their strengths in different circumstances and increases their total job satisfaction.

To apply job sculpting, you first need to identify the interests of your high performers. Then find creative opportunities for them to express their interests. For example, employees with an interest in managing people might enjoy scheduling the tasks of their subordinates. People who like to think creatively should enjoy participating in brainstorming sessions.

While it's always good management practice to match your employees' interests with the duties and tasks you assign to them, it's particularly important when it comes to retaining high performers. For high performers, work that's challenging and meaningful always aligns with their own interests and strengths.

As a manager, it's your task to identify the synergy that exists between your top performers' interests and strengths and the organization's overall goals and objectives.

In this way, you'll be able to steer your high performers toward tasks they excel at. And you'll maximize the contribution they make to the business.

The fifth technique you can use to develop the potential of your high performers is to use mentoring. In mentoring situations, an experienced person is paired with a less experienced person and provides guidance, encouragement, and instruction. Mentoring is often considered a way of grooming high performers for future success. Because they're often ambitious, they usually respond well to mentoring situations.

In order to mentor high performers successfully, ensure you pair them with mentors who can motivate and stimulate them, and spur them on to further achievement. Also, the mentoring itself should have a long-term focus.

Pair with mentors who motivate

In a mentoring relationship, high performers should be paired with senior executives who can motivate and inspire them, and groom them for career advancement.

In particular, having a mentor who has already attained the specific career goals and ambitions the person is working to achieve can be highly motivating for high performers. For example, a legal assistant who is training to become a lawyer could be paired with a mentor who successfully followed this route into the legal profession.

The mentor and high performer should get along well and be a good fit if the mentoring relationship is to be successful. For example, the mentor could have skills the high performer wants to learn.

Mentoring should have long-term focus

A mentor isn't responsible for managing a high performer's day-to-day activities. So a mentoring session shouldn't involve directing a person's actions at work, or coaching a person in how to perform various job-related tasks. This is the function of the person's supervisor, not a mentor. Instead, mentors should focus on the individual's career development and have a long-term focus.

For example, mentors could discover what high performers wants to achieve over the next five years and provide insight and support in helping them achieve their goals.

By using these five techniques, you'll get the most from your high performers. You'll motivate them to do great work. You'll also help them develop to their full potential, which should make it easier to retain them.

In this way, your high performers can continue to contribute to the success of your organization now and into the future.

Providing motivating feedback

High performers usually like to receive regular, detailed feedback about their performance. If you don't provide high performers with such feedback, they may feel they're not valued by the organization. This could cause them to feel demotivated or to resign.

Providing motivating feedback can help you retain the high performers in your organization. To provide motivating feedback, there are two principles to remember. First, you should look for ways to use feedback to build confidence in your high performers. And second, your feedback should provide them with guidance and freedom. However, it shouldn't provide detailed steps for them to follow.

Build confidence

The feedback you provide to high performers should build their confidence. They're usually the most self-critical employees, so it's important that you show your appreciation of their work, and encourage and reassure them. So compliment high performers when they do excellent work, and tell them how much you value the contribution they're making.

Be sincere in your compliments. High performers like honest, direct feedback that helps them do even more outstanding work. They also like feedback to be brief, specific, and to the point. So instead of just saying "Good job," say "Thanks so much for all your work on that last sale. You did a great job in discovering the customers' needs and meeting their concerns about service."

Provide guidance, not steps

High performers dislike being told what to do. They like the freedom of running their own projects and figuring out how to achieve their goals. They like to do things their way. So your feedback shouldn't prescribe to them, or impose rules or restrictions. Instead, it should guide them and give them options.

Avoid micromanaging high performers, as they dislike being "babysat." For example, don't oversee or dictate every small step they take. And don't make all their decisions for them. Your feedback should demonstrate that you trust them to do great work and to achieve the desired results.

If you micromanage high performers, they may feel you don't trust them. This could be demotivating for them, and might cause them to feel less valued.

Norma is the manager of the Creative Design Department in a large advertising agency. Today she's meeting with Ross, her best performer. Ross has just completed the artwork for a major new advertising campaign the agency is working on. Norma wants to provide him with motivating feedback on his recent performance and about his next assignment.

Follow along as Norma provides feedback to Ross in a way that motivates him and builds his confidence.

Norma: Well done, Ross. These advertisements for Poseidon Bank look fantastic.

Norma is happy.

Ross: Thanks. I was worried my idea about including historical images wouldn't work. But I think the overall composition of each advertisement is OK.

Ross is cautious.

Norma: This campaign is more than OK. Each advertisement is fresh and interesting. And you completed the campaign two weeks ahead of schedule, which is great.

Norma is encouraging.

Ross: Well, I enjoyed working on the campaign. I was able to throw myself into the project and be as creative as I liked.

Ross is positive.

Norma: This campaign is going to enhance the agency's reputation. I want you to know that I really value your work, Ross.

Norma is proud.

Ross: Great. It's good to know my work is appreciated. Ross is happy.

Norma: Now, regarding the Poseidon campaign, there's one thing I want to draw your attention to. Do you realize you went slightly over budget?

Norma is helpful.

Ross: No, I didn't realize that. I guess I was so wrapped up with designing the artwork that I didn't manage the budget as well as I should have. I'll keep a closer eye on the budget in the future.

Ross is surprised.

Norma: Thanks, Ross. Keep up the good work! Norma is encouraging.

Norma's feedback motivates Ross and builds his confidence. She expresses her feedback in a direct and encouraging way. She states how much she values his work, and her compliments are specific. And she tells Ross how to do even better in the future.

Norma then moves the discussion on to Ross's next assignment. Follow along as Norma provides feedback to Ross about the assignment in a way that offers guidance and freedom, but doesn't dictate the steps to follow.

Norma: I have an exciting new project for you, Ross. One of our biggest clients, Zoflina, has asked the agency to design a series of advertisements. It's a very lucrative contract, but the advertisements need to be delivered quickly. I want you to be the lead designer on the project.

Norma is enthusiastic.

Ross: That's fantastic news! I've always wanted to work on the Zoflina account. I can start work on this project right away. What would you like me to do first?

Ross is excited.

Norma: You need to come up with some creative ideas fast, and pitch them to the marketing people at Zoflina. Feel free to manage the design phase in whatever way suits you best – you're the creative expert, after all. Involve your colleagues when you need them. However you do it, just come up with some good designs.

Norma is encouraging.

Ross: That's fine. I'm happy to handle the design phase. I'll schedule a brainstorming session with our creative team tomorrow. I should have some initial designs mocked up and ready for you to review next week.

Ross is enthusiastic.

Norma: As soon as your designs are mocked up, call Zoflina and arrange a meeting with the marketing manager. I don't need to review your work first – I know I can trust you to do a good job.

Norma is confident.

Ross: OK, I'll do that – and I won't let you down. I know how important the Zoflina account is to the agency.

Ross is positive.

Norma: I know I can rely on you. Now, I'll give you some time and space to get started. I'll check in with you again at the end of the week. In the meantime, if you run into any problems, let me know.

Norma is trusting.

Ross: Thanks Norma. I can't wait to get working on this assignment. I've got some ideas already!

Ross is happy.

Norma's feedback about the new assignment motivates Ross. She provides him with the freedom to manage the assignment in his own way. She guides him, but doesn't tell him exactly which steps to follow. Norma also demonstrates that she's not micromanaging Ross, and that she trusts him to do a good job.

Learning Aid - Questions for Managers

To use this follow-on activity, consider the questions listed in the table. Then complete the table by filling in your answer to each question. You can print this document, or recreate the table in a word processing or spreadsheet application and use it to complete this activity.

The high performers in your organization are your greatest asset, and can have a major impact on revenues. Consider the questions about the high performers you manage. Use your answers to help you get the most from them.

1. Who are the high performers in your department or company?
2. Why do you recognize these people as high performers?

3. What characteristics do the high performers in your company share?
4. How big a role do you think your high performers will play in taking your organization to the next level of success?
5. How much of your company's present success can be attributed to its people?
6. How much of your company's present success can be attributed to its people?
7. Does your work culture value high performers? If so, in what ways?
8. What do your high performers think about the direction your organization is presently going in?
9. Do your high performers contribute to your company's policies?
10. Can you think of ways of increasing the impact high performers can make on your organization
11.

Learning Aid - **Characteristics of High Performers**

High performers usually share a number of key characteristics. Managers who understand these characteristics will find it easier to motivate and retain the high performers in their organizations.

Characteristic	How it's exhibited
High performers view work as more than a job	Regard work as a way to make a difference to the world, help others, or prove their own value
	Take their work very seriously
	Are completely focused on what they're doing
High performers exploit their strengths	Recognize their own inherent strengths and weaknesses
	Choose careers that exploit their strengths
High performers have clear goals	Tend to focus on results
	Are very ambitious
	Know where they're going in life and have a strategy for getting there
	Prefer to follow their own agendas
	May believe that company rules don't apply to them
	Use results-driven behavior that can sometimes come across as offensive, disrespectful, or rude
High performers have high expectations	Have high expectations of themselves and of others
	Frequently make demands on themselves and on the people around them
	Are more self-critical and impatient than the average employee
	Are more sensitive to dissatisfaction
High performers are enthusiastic about work	Like to generate joy and meaning from their occupations
	Believe in the wider benefit of what they're doing
High performers look for challenges and autonomy	Tend to get bored easily, so need to be challenged at work
	Like knowing that when one project ends, another challenge lies ahead
	Like to use all their talents to overcome challenges
	Yearn for responsibility and autonomy over their work
	Like to have complete ownership over what they're doing

Learning Aid - Techniques for Motivating and Developing High Performers

As a manager, you have the best chance of retaining high performers in your organization if you develop their potential and keep them motivated and happy.

Technique	How to Implement it
Reward fairly	Ensure high performers are rewarded and compensated fairly. But as financial reward isn't their main incentive, find other ways of rewarding them too.
	Offer them flexible and attractive working conditions.
	Find out what they want and do your best to meet their needs.
Provide meaningful, challenging work	Give high performers the opportunity to learn and use new skills. They like to feel they are developing and growing.
	Vary and rotate the roles they play, and engage them in the direction of the company.
	Ensure their goals are aligned to the overall corporate direction.
	Train them to be experts in their jobs.
Allow input	Tell high performers what to do, but not how to do it. They like to act independently and find innovative ways of doing things.
	Give them autonomy over how they perform their work, give them additional responsibility, and delegate tasks to them.
	State the results you want to see, set parameters for them, support them, and conduct progress reviews along the way.
Ensure roles emphasize strengths	Use job sculpting to ensure the tasks you assign to top performers emphasize their strengths. This allows them apply their strengths in different circumstances and increases job satisfaction.
	To apply job sculpting, first identify the interests of your high performers. Then find creative opportunities for them to express their interests.
	Identify the synergy that exists between your top performers' interests and strengths, and the organization's overall goals and objectives.
Use mentoring	High performers are usually very ambitious, and respond well to mentoring. They should be mentored by senior executives who can motivate and inspire them.
	Mentors should focus on the individual's career development and have a long-term focus.

CHAPTER FIVE
Managing New Managers

Managing New Managers

A new manager can include a person who has been hired from outside the company, or it could be a person who has received a promotion from within the company. Both types of managers need to undergo orientation to make a smooth transition.

Providing orientation for new managers entails three key actions. The first is recognizing the importance of new manager orientation. The second is determining the appropriate content of the orientation. The third action is addressing cultural sensitivity issues.

Training plays an important part in a manager's development. By receiving the correct training, new managers are being prepared to exert a positive influence over their departments or sections.

There are several techniques for training new managers: coaching, job shadowing, involving new manager in shared projects, personal study, organizing customer and supplier visits, setting up briefings or presentations, and using the Internet and e-learning.

Companies use mentoring programs so that new managers can benefit from observing how experienced managers lead and manage people. There are three steps in the mentoring model: first, assess the current situation; second, explore ideal options; and third, develop a plan and take action.

New manager orientation

Orienting yourself simply means adjusting to and becoming familiar with your new surroundings. For example, hikers use maps to figure out what direction to travel in and how to return home. When a manager is new to a company or has received an internal promotion, an orientation process helps make the manager's transition into the team a lot smoother.

There are three key areas to consider in the orientation process. The first is knowing the importance of new manager orientation. The second is awareness of the content of the orientation. And the final consideration is addressing cultural sensitivity issues.

Recognizing the importance of new manager orientation can help when it comes to the issue of retaining talented employees. There's a lot of competition between companies to recruit the best managerial candidates.

That's why companies need to continually sell the job to new managers. Sometimes, new managers can experience new manager remorse – uncertainty and doubt about their new position.

An effective new manager orientation process should allow for this uncertainty and provide effective countermeasures to ensure the person is reassured and positively engaged in the new position.

One of the best ways you can successfully integrate new managers is by aiming to create a dynamic, motivational atmosphere in which they can excel.

When an orientation process includes this aim, it's positively working to remove the element of doubt a new manager might be experiencing. When the right atmosphere is created, a new manager is less likely to experience anxiety over accepting the new position.

During the orientation process, you should make it clear to the new manager what the benefits of working with the company are. By selling the employee on the positive aspects associated with growing with the company, the person is less likely to leave.

Recognizing the importance of new manager orientation not only involves continually selling the job and creating a dynamic, motivational atmosphere, it entails spreading the right message. Orientation presents an opportunity for a company to articulate the values needed to be successful. Every company's orientation policy should provide a platform for employees to learn about a company's culture, its strategic aims, and its internal and external operating practices.

Content and cultural considerations

The second aspect of new manager orientation is to carefully consider what the content of the orientation will be. You can use the orientation process to provide the new manager with the basic information, skills, and tools needed to perform well.

The orientation should provide the new manager with a clear picture of the company's organizational structure, and where the manager's department is located within it.

New managers need to know what role their departments will play in executing a company's strategy. Of equal importance for new managers is understanding how their departments' operations can have a positive or negative impact on other departments within the company.

To achieve this objective, a new manager should be able to meet with existing company leaders to discuss alignment, strategy, the potential for cooperation, and how to avoid conflict.

For new managers, the content of the orientation should outline the specifics of how training is provided. This includes information about when training is to be provided, how it is to be given, and how much training there will be.

Ideally, training is provided in a time frame that allows instruction to take place in the most concise and comprehensive way possible. Training can be broken down into individual day-long modules.

These sessions shouldn't all run together. By providing breaks, new managers will have time to absorb the newly acquired information and consider how to use that information on the job.

New managers need to receive training in four general management-related areas, in addition to more specialized training related to their respective roles. These four areas are contractual information, employee relations, interview etiquette, and delegation.

Contractual information

New managers should be aware of the legal procedures that govern contractual negotiations. This includes labor contractual negotiations and contracts involving suppliers or customers.

Employee relations

When moving into a position of authority, new managers may find that colleagues will have a different attitude toward them. Managers need to be able to handle these situations in a professional manner.

Interview etiquette

Interviewing applicants for vacancies is a managerial task. New managers should be familiar with the legal aspects involved to avoid potential lawsuits. In addition, managers need to learn how to match the right person with the right job.

Delegation

Delegating is one of the most common tasks a manager will carry out. New managers need to be taught the correct delegation techniques that have previously worked in the company.

There are various topics that should be addressed in the first week of orientation to allow a new manager to begin working:
- reviewing vision and mission statements
- reviewing health and safety requirements
- training on systems a new manager needs working knowledge of
- defining roles and functions of a manager, and
- training on cultural sensitivities

However, even though the first week of orientation is important, the process should be viewed as ongoing, extending beyond a few weeks.

Once a new manager has been put in place, feedback sessions should be scheduled and performance evaluations carried out.

A company should begin to plan a new manager's development by identifying potential growth and learning opportunities the manager can avail of in the future.

The third aspect of new manager orientation is addressing cultural sensitivity issues. Remember that new managers may come from different countries and have different cultural backgrounds. The person supervising the orientation should realize that people from different backgrounds may process information differently, and some people may be uncomfortable with certain approaches to training and group meetings.

Orientations should embrace and cater to different cultures. For instance, some managers will come from an egalitarian background, while others come from a more hierarchical background.

Again, depending on their backgrounds, some new managers may have a formal or informal managerial style. Or they may have a direct or indirect communication style.

Some cultures welcome a group-based approach, while others take an individualist approach. What must be remembered is that all cultural groups deserve equal respect in the workplace.

Providing training for new managers

Successful managers regard their careers as a long learning process. They become more effective as they gain additional experience. Training plays an important part in a manager's development. New managers, in particular, benefit from training techniques that develop their leadership capabilities. By receiving the appropriate leadership training, managers can guide and motivate employees to become more productive and effective.

Companies provide new managers with proper training because it can help them develop effective leadership styles. New managers should be results-oriented and people-focused. This combination allows them to get the best from their teams and deliver bottom-line results for their companies.

New managers are groomed to become the future leaders of their companies. Strong leadership is one of the most important competitive advantages a company can have. Leaders create strategies and vision, and they build their companies' resources to achieve corporate goals.

However, bad leadership can be the worst liability for companies. When companies run into difficulties, it's usually because of poor performance, which stems from ineffective leadership.

That's why companies value leadership development training. This training can equip managers with the tools and know-how to enable them to begin the journey to becoming successful leaders.

For today's new managers to become the leaders of tomorrow, they must go through an effective training program that covers several elements: general training, mandatory training, job training, and training evaluation.

General training

General training provides instruction regarding a company's values and corporate philosophy. It also outlines the company's structure and its history.

Mandatory training

Mandatory training covers areas relating to legislative compliance. It includes health and safety training as well as information about workers' rights.

Job training

Job training relates specifically to the role the new manager will be taking on. This training provides the manager with the necessary skills to begin the role.

Training evaluation

Training evaluation is the process in which the new manager's understanding of the role, and the person's ability to carry it out, is assessed. The evaluation also includes feedback sessions. In addition, the trainee's thoughts regarding the overall training experience are solicited.

New manager training techniques

There are numerous training techniques that you can use to develop new managers' leadership capabilities. The seven principle techniques are coaching; job shadowing; involving the new manager in shared projects; personal study; customer and supplier visits; setting up briefings and presentations; and Internet and e-learning.

The first training technique, coaching, is perhaps the most fundamental for developing the leadership possibilities of new managers.

When providing the training for new managers, you need to develop a leadership model that the trainees can recognize and understand. This leadership model should convey to the new managers what type of person they should look for as a role model and, if possible, suggest people within the company that fit this model.

Coaching also involves encouraging and nurturing new managers. By encouraging new managers to take risks and look beyond conventional management methods, coaches are producing more dynamic leaders. By nurturing them, a coach discovers what unique skills and abilities each person has. The coach then works with the new managers to further develop these talents so that they can be applied to each manager's new role.

For example, Elke is a training specialist with a large biopharmaceutical company. She has been asked to provide training for a group of new business managers who are about to be deployed across several of the company's departments. Some of the trainees have been promoted from within the company, while some were hired from outside.

To apply the coaching technique, Elke explains what abilities, experience, and traits the company likes its managers to have. She provides a senior manager's contact information in each trainee's respective department and encourages the trainees to make contact.

Elke encourages and mentors the new trainees by scheduling time to have one-on-one chats with each of them. During these meetings, she suggests that the trainees take risks. She also learns about their individual talents. Elke strongly suggests that they should look for opportunities to incorporate these talents into their new roles.

Job shadowing is the second technique. It allows trainees to observe experienced managers carrying out their duties.

The new managers get to view a real-time, on-the-job demonstration of what is required of them once their training is completed. In many cases, trainees are invited by those they are observing to demonstrate their understanding of these skills.

Returning to the example of Elke, she makes sure there is time in each new manager's training schedule to shadow experienced managers.

Elke explains that job shadowing can help the new manager to understand company practices, as well as to develop new relationships.

It can also help the manager understand departmental interactions as well as all the different functions within the company.

Understand company practices

Job shadowing can develop a new manager's understanding of the standard operating practices and procedures of a company. Seeing these being carried out in a real working environment will help the new manager remember and understand them better.

Develop relationships

By shadowing colleagues as they carry out their duties, new managers will be able to forge important relationships with the person they're observing. In addition, they'll meet other colleagues through the person they are shadowing. This will help establish future working relationships.

Understand departmental interactions

Job shadowing allows a new manager to observe how different departments and functions interact with each other. The new manager will also be able to gain an insight into the internal workings of each department. This will be very beneficial when the manager begins working with a specific department.

Involving new managers in shared projects is the third training technique. New managers get the opportunity to be actively involved in one of the company's projects. This enables them to develop their own team building skills by seeing experienced managers interacting with members of their teams. They will also experience how each team, or project group, interacts with each other.

For instance, Elke assigns the new managers to a team that's working on marketing one of the company's products in foreign markets.

The new managers observe the marketing manager lead the team, and they also get to play an active role themselves.

Because of the nature of the project, the marketing team interacts with both the sales team and the production team. Elke's trainees experience the full benefit of being involved in shared projects.

Personal study is the fourth training technique. Training is an ideal opportunity to convey the company's message to new managers. They should be provided with reading material that includes the company's mission statement, code of ethics, and corporate goals. New managers should also be knowledgeable of the industry that they're working in, who the company is competing with, and who the company's main customers are. It's important that they take the time to become familiar with this information.

To use the personal study technique, Elke uploads material about the company and the biopharmaceutical industry to USB flash drives. She presents a USB to each new manager when training begins. She makes it clear to them that it's their own responsibility to read the information.

Organizing customer and supplier visits is the fifth technique used for training new managers. It's likely that a new manager's department will have some level of customer and supplier interaction.

So it's important that a new manager is comfortable in dealing with customers and suppliers, and able to establish relationships with them. A new manager should know what these parties expect from the company and be able to resolve potential conflicts.

For example, Elke asks each new manager to make appointments with both a customer and a supplier of the respective departments that they have been allocated to. She asks the new managers to introduce themselves and begin establishing a working rapport with the suppliers and customers.

Setting up briefings and presentations is the sixth training technique that can benefit new managers.

By learning how to schedule and then give a briefing or presentation, new managers will be able to gain valuable information in an informal setting. They will also be able to use the briefing or presentation situation to ask relevant questions and address issues or concerns.

For example, to ensure that the new managers with the biopharmaceutical company are comfortable doing this, Elke asks each one to give a presentation or briefing – about a relevant biopharmaceutical issue – to the whole training group. The new manager then asks questions and answers any in return.

The final technique for training new managers involves the use of the Internet and e-learning. In many instances, new managers will need to receive training while they're actually working in their new roles. The Internet and e-learning provide new managers with the opportunity to take advantage of training sessions from their desktop at work or at home.

In this example, some members of Elke's training group have been fast-tracked into their new roles because of an increase in demand for some of the company's products.

These individuals still need to receive training in different areas.

Elke creates a link on the company's intranet where she posts recordings of training presentations and notes for the new managers to access when they get the chance.

Benefits of mentoring new managers

Sometimes new managers find it difficult to reach their full potential. They may not have sufficient experience to immediately become good leaders. This is why some companies use mentoring programs. A senior manager acts as a mentor to a new manager, who then benefits from observing how the more experienced manager leads and manages people. The mentor has already dealt with the challenges that the mentee now faces, so the mentor can positively guide, inform, and influence the new manager.

Mentoring is a key technique for bringing out the best in new managers. An experienced manager can encourage the development of a new manager by sharing expertise, perspective, resources, and skills.

The relationship between mentor and mentee benefits both parties. The mentor's abilities and skills are enhanced by the continual reassessment involved in the mentoring process, while the mentee's knowledge, abilities, and career development progress.

Good mentors need to have a number of attributes. These can be categorized as either professional attributes or personal attributes.

Professional attributes

Effective mentors are willing to share professional life experiences at a management level. Mentors should be trustworthy and respected within the company and the industry. A mentor should be able to provide constructive criticism and respect confidentiality.

Personal attributes

Effective mentors take a caring approach when dealing with mentees. Their demeanor is empathetic and respectful, and their actions are conducted with integrity. They're enthusiastic and motivational, open and positive, and good listeners.

Consider this example of a mentoring relationship. Chris is a senior manager with a recruitment company. He's been asked to mentor Tony, a new manager who's just been hired.

Tony immediately begins to learn from Chris. He finds out that their company provides workforce solutions for clients in the manufacturing industry. Tony is introduced to many of these important clients.

Chris explains the company's approach to finding potential employees to recommend to its clients. He shows Tony how to cross reference the company's extensive database of individuals looking for work and how to select the people with the right skills for each job.

Chris tells Tony about his own background with the company. He discusses how he started out as an office administrator and worked his way up to upper management, where he underwent a mentoring process as well.

Chris explains that he was encouraged by the company to work hard and develop new skills. He says he was pleased to find the company recognized talent and ambition, and this is why he's stayed with the company for so long.

Tony mentions to Chris that he has several qualifications in human resources management. Chris is impressed and says that the company always needs people with this type of experience and know-how.

Tony finds Chris to be very approachable and knowledgeable. Being mentored by Chris has been an inspirational experience for him. Tony now knows that the company provides opportunities for personal and professional development. He's determined to make the most of these opportunities.

Assessing the current situation

There are several different ways to develop a mentoring program within a company. This topic focuses on a three-phase model of mentoring. Step one in the model is to assess the current situation. Step two is to explore ideal options, and step three is to develop a plan and take action.

The first step in the mentoring process is to assess the current situation. During this phase, the mentor encourages the mentee to open up and listens actively to what the mentee says. The mentor also helps the mentee reach a new perspective on a situation and frames a problem in a manageable way.

To get a mentee to open up, you need to provide a comfortable and safe environment. In some cases, new managers find it difficult to discuss certain subjects or admit their own failings. Choose a meeting place that you know the mentee will feel relaxed in. By creating the right environment, you make it easier for new managers to discuss issues they face.

You can ask open questions to prompt discussion. For example, you might ask new managers what their professional goals and personal ambitions are. Avoid using an impatient or terse tone when asking questions.

Effective mentors pay close attention to responses and paraphrase to clarify understanding where necessary.

To help mentees reach new perspectives on situations, mentors first adopt an empathetic approach. A mentor discusses what the mentee has said, then offers a different take on the situation to get the new manager to consider it from a different angle.

This approach also helps new managers overcome blind spots. By talking issues through with their mentors, new managers can start to see things from their colleagues' perspectives.

A mentor can frame a problem in a manageable way by initially asking questions such as, "How do you feel about it?" or "What are you thinking?" The mentor then asks questions that are more detailed – for example "What exactly is the problem for you?" or "How do others view the situation?" This approach helps the mentee consider the problem in a logical manner.

Consider this example of what's involved in the first step in the mentoring process, assessing the current situation. Celeste is a senior manager with an e-marketing company. She has several years of experience with the company.

She has been asked to mentor Marvin, a new manager. Marvin's previous experience was in print-based direct marketing. He's finding the transition to an e-marketing environment difficult.

Follow along as Celeste assesses Marvin's situation.

Celeste: Marvin, thanks for agreeing to have this meeting in my office. The main open-plan office where you're based can be hectic sometimes. The reason I asked to speak with you is that I think you've been under a lot of pressure recently. I wanted to check that you're OK. Celeste is friendly.

Marvin: Well, I guess there's always going to be an adjustment period when you start a new job. But I'm getting along fine. Thanks for asking, though.

Marvin is uncomfortable.

Celeste: It seems to me that you're experiencing difficulty in getting your team to carry out your instructions.

Celeste is sympathetic.

Marvin: There's some truth to that. I think my team regards my background as being slightly out of date for e-marketing.

Marvin is agitated.

Celeste: This situation could happen to any new manager joining the company. Try not to take it personally. Let's focus on your professional goals. Can you tell me what you hope to achieve in your career?

Celeste is interested.

Marvin: I want to be a success with this company. I moved from print-based direct marketing to e-marketing because I believe this is where the future of the industry is. And I want to start new trends in e-marketing, rather than to follow old ones.

Marvin is eager.

Celeste: That's good to hear. We need ambitious and innovative people. You've said that your team might not respect your background. Have you tried explaining to them how successful you were in your old job? You don't have to boast, but if you outline your role in some successful projects, your team might begin to listen.

Celeste is helpful.

Marvin: No, I haven't discussed my previous experience with the team.

Marvin is agreeing.

Celeste: Have you considered the situation from the team's point of view? Have you told them about your desire to become an innovative leader in the e-marketing industry? They're ambitious as well. Perhaps you need to show them that you're the manager who will allow them to achieve their goals.

Celeste is encouraging.

Exploring ideal options

The second step in the mentoring process is to explore ideal options. Once the new manager's problem has been identified, the mentor can assist the mentee in creating the ideal scenario. To do this effectively, the mentor facilitates brainstorming and defines realistic goals.

A mentor facilitates brainstorming by encouraging the new manager to think as imaginatively as possible. This involves encouraging the new manager to use creative thinking. By asking a mentee to consider imaginative solutions rather than solutions constrained by practicalities, new energy and enthusiasm can be generated.

The mentor shouldn't be too judgmental of the new manager's proposed solutions. To criticize at this point could compromise or impede the mentee's openness and honesty.

Once the new manager starts suggesting ideas and solutions, the mentor should ask questions to keep the flow of ideas moving. Suitable prompting questions include, "What is your ideal situation?" and "What might you be thinking and feeling during this ideal situation?"

Remember Celeste and Marvin? Now that they've identified that Marvin has a problem getting respect from his team, they begin to work on finding solutions. Celeste asks Marvin to consider his ideal situation. He replies that it would involve his team accepting his ideas and working hard to implement his e-marketing strategies.

Celeste realizes that Marvin's ideal situation would be hard to completely replicate in reality. She knows that team members will disagree and have their own working preferences. But she doesn't criticize the idea because she doesn't want to interrupt Marvin's thought process.

She knows that they can work toward achieving as much of his ideal situation as they possibly can. She prompts Marvin by asking a series of follow-up questions about how he would feel if this situation was a reality. She also asks him how his team members would feel if he explained his ideal situation to them.

Defining realistic goals is another important action to take when exploring ideal options. To do this, the mentor and mentee work together to draw up a list of SMART aims based on what they have discussed so far. SMART stands for specific, measurable, attainable, realistic, and timely. A collaborative approach is much more effective than if you just give the mentee goals that you have identified.

Specific

A specific aim or goal is more likely to be achieved than a general one. The best way for a mentee to set a specific goal is to ask a series of questions: Who's involved? What needs to be accomplished? and Why does it need to be accomplished?

Celeste and Marvin run through these questions. Marvin and his team are involved. Marvin wants to get the respect of his team. This is required because the current situation is negatively affecting Marvin's performance, as well as the team's.

Measurable

The criteria for measuring whether an aim has been achieved should be made clear. By measuring progress, a mentee can keep to the schedule and know when the aim has been achieved.

Celeste and Marvin decide to use weekly meetings to discuss Marvin's progress as he strives to gain his team's respect.

Attainable

Different skills and resources will be required to accomplish an aim. Most goals are attainable when properly prepared for.

Celeste suggests that Marvin study team building techniques, conflict management skills, and motivational approaches in his spare time. This will better prepare him to attain his goal.

Realistic

A realistic aim is an objective that a person wants to achieve and is able to achieve. It's the individual's choice about how high to set the aim.

Marvin identifies his aim: to gain the respect of his team. This goal is something he wants to achieve and he knows that he has the ability to do so.

Timely

An aim should be achieved within a pre-determined time frame. This will motivate the person to carry out the necessary tasks to succeed.

Celeste knows that Marvin's aim can't be achieved quickly. It will require constant effort on his part over a prolonged period of time. However, she also knows that the company can't afford to tolerate a dysfunctional team for a long time. She and Marvin decide to set a time frame of two months for him to make significant progress.

Once it's been decided what the SMART aims are, the mentor should ask questions to ensure the mentee is committed to achieving these aims. These questions are designed to make the mentee aware of both the benefits and the risks of trying to achieve them.

Celeste asks Marvin how he expects to benefit from gaining his team's respect. She also asks him what he's willing to give up to achieve this. She's satisfied that Marvin's responses represent a complete commitment to accomplishing his goal.

Developing a plan and taking action

After the mentor and mentee complete the second step in the mentoring model by defining the problem and suggesting ways to make improvements, they move on to the third step – develop a plan and take action. This involves considering what resources are needed and facilitating action planning.

Considering what resources are needed is an essential part of executing the plan. Resources could include people, places, assets, other companies, training plans, or anything else that's necessary to complete the plan. The mentee should carefully consider each resource. People, for instance, could mean a person that supports the mentee's idea.

When the plan is finalized, it's time for the mentee to act. To facilitate action planning, the mentor helps the mentee to analyze the plan, break it down into manageable tasks, and set time frames for each task. The mentor maintains an active role and follows the mentee's progress.

Celeste's mentee Marvin has identified people as his main resource. He knows that some members of his team are supportive, while others aren't. He decides that he needs to work with both groups to retain the support of one and gain the support of the other.

Marvin presents his final plan to Celeste. She approves its content and allocates a time period for each objective to be completed within.

Learning Aid - **Rate Your Mentoring Potential**

You can print this document, or recreate the table in a word processing or spreadsheet application and use it to complete this activity.

Rate your potential as a mentor by selecting your level of ability using each technique. When you are finished, study your selections and work on the techniques that you have rated as "adequate" or "need to improve."

Technique	Good	Adequate	Need to improve
Guide mentee to open up			
Listen actively to what mentee says			
Help mentee reach new perspective			
Frame problem in manageable way			
Facilitate brainstorming			
Avoid being judgmental			
Keep prompting			
Define realistic goals			
Ask appropriate questions			
Consider what resources are needed			
Facilitate action planning			

Learning Aid - **The First Week of Orientation**

During a new manager's first week of orientation, the following actions should be carried out:
- Review contractual information Review employee relations
- Review interview etiquette
- Review vision and mission statements Review health and safety policy

- Begin training on systems the new manager will need working knowledge of
- Define the roles and functions of a manager
- Provide training on cultural sensitivities

Learning Aid - Training Techniques

Technique	Description
Coaching	This technique should create a leadership model that conveys to new managers what type of person they should look for as a role model and, if possible, suggest people within the company that fit this model. Coaching also involves encouraging and nurturing new managers.
Job shadowing	Job shadowing allows trainees to observe experienced managers carrying out their duties. The new managers get to view a real-time, on-the-job demonstration of what is required of them once their training is completed. In many cases, trainees are invited by those they are observing to demonstrate their understanding of these skills.
Involving in shared projects	New managers get the opportunity to be actively involved in one of the company's projects. This enables them to develop their own team building skills by seeing experienced managers interacting with members of their teams, and how each team, or project group, interacts with each other.
Assign personal study	Training is an ideal opportunity to convey the company's message to new managers. They should be provided with reading material that includes the company's mission statement, code of ethics, and corporate goals. New managers should also be knowledgeable of the industry that they are working in, who the company is competing with, and who the company's main customers are.
Customer and supplier visits	It's important that a new manager is comfortable in dealing with customers and suppliers, and able to establish relationships with them. A new manager should know what these parties expect from the company, and be able to resolve potential conflicts.
Setting up briefings and presentations	By learning how to schedule and then give a briefing or presentation, new managers will gain valuable information in an informal setting. They will also be able to use the briefing or presentation situation to ask relevant questions and address issues or concerns.
Internet and e-learning	Internet and e-learning provide new managers with the opportunity to avail of training sessions from their desktop from work or from home. Companies can develop their own in-house Internet and e-learning capabilities or subcontract the task to an external organization.

CHAPTER SIX
Managing Experienced Managers

Managing Experienced Managers

Investing in managers is an important strategic aspect of managing experienced managers. There are six techniques for investing in managers: working to gain their commitment to the organization's vision, improving culture and supporting positive values, valuing their experience and insights, allowing them more autonomy, motivating them, and developing a succession plan.

There are four stages in the coaching process. The first stage is determination. This stage allows you to assess whether coaching is appropriate. If so, you'll have an initial meeting to clarify how the coaching will move forward over the agreed time frame.

The second stage of the coaching process is to create an action plan. This should be a joint effort between you and the manager. The third stage is implementation, where the manager has an opportunity to practice skills. Finally, an assessment will determine the extent to which the action plan has been successful.

In this topic, you will understand facilitating an initial coaching meeting with an experienced manager. The key elements of the initial coaching session are to begin the session positively, link any critical feedback to the effects on others and the organization, and establish clearly defined goals.

There are many techniques for assessing a manager's performance. You can observe the manager's availability and approachability, and interview the manager's direct reports by walking around. You can gather evidence by reviewing the manager's calendar and daily activities and looking out for telltale signs of bad management. Finally, look out for whether the manager focuses too much on the team rather than the organization.

When managing nonperformers, you should deal with the problem immediately and hold the manager accountable for low performance. Make your expectations clear and keep a performance log. Then work with the manager to search for solutions to problems. Finally, follow up with the manager regularly to review progress.

Investing in managers

As an experienced people manager, you've probably developed many management skills. However, managing experienced managers requires you to redirect your focus. You should be focused on formulating and implementing strategy, effective communication, and building managers as managers.

Three key aspects of managing managers are worth emphasizing. First, you must invest in management talent.

Second, you need to coach experienced managers to develop their potential.

Finally, it's necessary to tackle problem performance in managers where it occurs. The first strategy, investing in management talent, will be covered in this topic.

Investing in management talent is a key strategic aspect of managing your managers effectively. This requires an understanding of what motivates each manager. Although compensation is important, other factors are equally significant to managers. Examples include opportunities for personal and career growth, and the chance to make a contribution to the organization.

There are six techniques for investing in your management talent. Make an effort to gain their commitment to the organization's vision. Improve your organization's culture. Let them know that you value their experience and insights. Allow them more autonomy where possible. Motivate them, but think beyond financial incentives. And finally, develop a succession plan.

Gain commitment to vision

Unfocused employees are usually unhappy employees. They may lose interest in their roles. This is especially relevant when managing managers. If they're unfocused and uninterested, it sets a bad example for their direct reports.

Managers may be committed to a vision, but if they don't fully understand what the vision is, they may be wasting their efforts. Managers higher up should ensure that the vision is both properly communicated and accepted by the managers below them.

Improve culture and support positive values

An organization's culture is the behavior and interaction of individuals and groups within the organization. It's reflected in the leadership structure, systems, and processes. Simply put, it's "the ways things are done around here."

You're an integral part of your organization's culture. You influence the perceptions of your direct reports and their teams. This is a position of influence that should be used wisely to improve the cultural experience and support positive values.

Value experience and insights

Valuing your managers' experience and insights will help them feel connected with the organization. This will give them a sense of ownership and help to retain their commitment to the organization.

Allow more autonomy

Higher levels of autonomy in the workplace have been shown to increase job satisfaction and, in many cases, motivation to perform the job. Allowing managers more autonomy will likely make them feel they're making a difference to the organization's success.

Think beyond financial incentives

Financial incentives include cash bonuses, increased pay, and stock or stock options. However, managers are often more motivated by nonfinancial rewards, such as opportunities for personal growth.

Develop a succession plan

Succession planning is a process for identifying and developing managers with the potential to fill key leadership positions in the organization.

Succession plans give experienced managers opportunities to further develop their competencies to reach expectations. A good plan allows them to put themselves forward as potential candidates to fill higher management positions as these become available.

A good way to gain commitment to the company's vision is to introduce short-term and long-term business plans that are aligned with the organization's vision and values. Short-term business plans with measurable outcomes – such as monthly sales targets – would allow managers to gauge their progress. Managers would also see how they're contributing to the organization. Long-term plans – such as a three year resource plan – would allow managers to make decisions in the context of the organization's long-term vision.

The second technique for investing in managers is to improve culture and support positive values. Improving managers' experiences of organizational culture can motivate them. A positive work environment is more likely to encourage managers to stay with the organization. If you play an active role in connecting your managers to organizational values, they'll be more committed to your organization.

One way to achieve this is to allow people to feel they're making a difference. Continuously matching individual attributes, skills, and needs with the organization can help individuals feel connected and useful. This is called the person-environment fit.

For example, say your marketing manager, Mike, expresses boredom with his current role. You could perhaps suggest a cross-functional project with the product development team to stimulate his creativity.

The third technique for investing in managers is to let them know you value their experience and insights. You may want to encourage managers to become mentors, solicit their help in developing training programs, ask for their opinions in various matters, and involve them in overall strategy development. Set up regular meetings with individual managers and teams of managers. This will allow you to review progress toward goals and give managers an opportunity to provide input in longer-term planning.

The fourth technique for investing in managers is to allow more autonomy. Increased autonomy should make managers feel a greater responsibility for the outcomes of their work, which will lead to an increase in motivation.

You can delegate and give managers more autonomy by involving them in as much decision-making in their areas of responsibility as possible. For example, you could give a manager responsibility for a project, resource planning, hiring new employees, budgets, or client management.

The fifth technique is to motivate your managers, particularly by thinking beyond financial incentives. For example, as many managers tend to actively manage their own careers, they often look for career progression through increasingly challenging assignments.

You could give managers a chance to lead a project that will give them recognition and opportunities to learn new skills. Other learning opportunities include secondment, external study programs, or internal management courses. Recognize managers by verbalizing your appreciation for their commitment.

The last technique, developing succession plans, should form part of a continuous performance assessment program within the organization. Setting clear objectives is critical to establishing effective succession planning.

To develop a succession plan, you could ask managers about their career plans, and work to build their objectives accordingly. You can then provide them with the opportunities and skills necessary to achieve their goals.

Benefits to coaching managers

Coaching is an important development tool used by many organizations to improve the capabilities of experienced managers. Coaching helps managers improve their performance through self-reflection and gives them opportunities to apply specific skills and knowledge.

There are four key characteristics of coaching. First, coaching focuses on meeting goals. Second, it's a long-term process designed for each manager based on individual experiences and past performance. Third, coaching seeks to achieve a balance between personal and organizational goals. And fourth, coaching encourages accountability in managers.

Consider Ayana, the managing director at an investment company. She's presenting to some of the company's shareholders and must justify the rationale behind spending money on coaching managers.

She discusses the coaching program, which gives managers time away from their daily responsibilities to undergo an assessment of their personal strengths and weaknesses. Each manager is matched to a personal coach from the senior management team. That coach then holds development meetings with the manager on a weekly basis.

She explains that coaching gives managers an opportunity to turn performance weaknesses into personal development opportunities. Furthermore, each coach is available to offer fresh ideas about current challenges, and identify areas of the business where the managers' skills and experience could be best used. One year into the program, senior managers have noted a significant improvement in their coachees' performance and an increase in productivity.

Determination and initial meeting

There are four key stages to the coaching process. The initial stage determines if coaching is appropriate. Second, if coaching is deemed appropriate, the coach and the manager create an action plan. The third step is to implement the action plan. The final step is an assessment of the action plan.

The first stage of the coaching process – the determination stage – has two important parts. You must begin by determining if coaching is appropriate. If you determine that it is, then you'll have an initial meeting with the manager.

Coaching is about improving performance by reflecting on the manager's current skills and knowledge. So before deciding whether coaching is appropriate, you'll have to observe the potential coachee, both formally and informally. You need to find out which skills exist, and which are needed.

You must be able to answer "yes" to a number of questions for coaching to be appropriate:
- Does the person already have the skill or knowledge to perform the job?

- Will the person be performing the task in the short-term?
- If you work with this person on a one-on-one basis, are you able to help improve the relevant aspect of the person's performance?
- Do you and the potential coachee have the time to commit to coaching?

Once coaching has been deemed appropriate, an initial meeting is crucial to establish the ongoing coaching process. Active listening is particularly important for a productive start to a coaching relationship based on trust and respect. For example, paraphrasing a colleague's dialogue can demonstrate that you've been listening attentively.

It's advisable to begin the first coaching session by providing positive comments and constructive criticism gleaned from your observations. When giving feedback, avoid suppositions about the manager's character. It's also important to relate critical feedback to the effect on others and the organization.

Even at the initial stages, it's best to agree on goals. You should clearly define the goals and state the benefits of achieving them. Then, for transparency and accountability, you should formally agree on the goals, as well as any desired competencies and time lines.

Ross has agreed to coach Lucy after determining their suitability as coach and coachee. They're having an initial meeting to lay down the foundation of the coaching relationship. Follow along as Ross opens the initial coaching meeting with Lucy.

Ross: Hi Lucy, thanks for meeting with me today. I'd like to begin by saying that I'm delighted we're going to be working together. You have an excellent reputation, and I hope I can help you achieve your goals. I do hear, however, that you're struggling to cope with the demands of your team? There have been a number of significant errors and client complaints.

Ross is happy.

Lucy: Thanks Ross. I think your experience can really help me deal with the challenges in my team. Yes, I'm having difficulty managing the workload. I feel like my team and my peers are pulling me in different directions.

Lucy is uncomfortable.

Ross: So what you'd like to get out of these coaching sessions is advice on how to delegate effectively within your team? And also how to manage your peers?

Ross is confident.

Lucy: Yes, that's exactly what I'd like to work on! Lucy is relieved.

Ross: OK, I can help you with that. I have extensive experience managing teams across the organization. What we need to do now is clarify achievable goals for you in the short term. We'll also establish some long-term goals. These goals will help motivate you to delegate more effectively on an ongoing basis.

Ross is confident.

Lucy: Great. So, should we just have a chat about it every week when we meet to see how I'm progressing?

Lucy is unsure.

Ross: We can actually add these goals to the company's online performance management system. Any time you encounter a relevant situation, you can update your progress against the goal. As your coach, I can regularly monitor any updates you add to the system.

Ross is confident.

Lucy: OK, great – that will really help me keep track of my progress!

Lucy is happy.

Create an action plan

The second stage in the coaching process is to create an action plan. The plan should include development targets and strategies to meet these targets. The targets should align with organizational goals. It's important to formulate the plan with the manager, rather than presenting it as a "done deal." If others are involved in the plan and need to be informed, only communicate the relevant parts of the plan to them; the coaching sessions should remain confidential.

There are several items to consider when developing an action plan with the manager:
- review each objective
- take account of the time available for coaching
- consider preliminary tasks the manager needs to perform, and
- consider whether others will be involved

Review each objective

When reviewing each objective, it's necessary to consider what the objective means, and what activities need to take place in order to achieve the objective. You should also determine when activities need to happen, especially if they relate to specific tasks on the manager's calendar. For example, will the manager have the opportunity to practice a development task in real life, or will a simulation be required?

Take account of time available

Time frames are necessary to monitor and assess the objectives. Time should be set aside for regular meetings between the coach and coachee. Overall time frames should be set for the coaching process – for example, one year. Then milestones should be agreed upon. These could perhaps be monthly or quarterly.

Consider preliminary tasks

The action plan should include acknowledgment of the performance gap – that is, the gap between the manager's current performance and desired performance. Inevitably, the manager will need to complete some preliminary tasks, such as formal classroom training, online training, refresher reading, or data collection. Also, some equipment or resources may be required for the manager to complete certain tasks.

Consider others

In many cases, the topics of the coaching sessions will involve other people. For example, the manager may want improved public presentation skills. Or the manager could wish to be more assertive in meetings. A desire to give better feedback to direct reports would also require consideration of others.

Implementation and assessment

The third stage of the coaching process is implementing the action plan. During this stage you must organize some experience so the manager can practice the performance objectives – for example, by carrying out a specific task.

Remember Ross and Lucy? Ideally, Lucy would practice her new skills in a real-life environment where Ross could observe her. Alternatively, Ross could arrange for Lucy to shadow another manager or participate in a role-playing activity. If it isn't practical for Ross to observe Lucy, then she should report back to Ross on her skills practice, and add notes to the performance plan.

The fourth and final stage in the coaching process is assessment. It's necessary to discuss the outcome of the action plan, including what was and wasn't achieved, key successes, and any constructive feedback on how the manager approached the tasks.

It's important for the manager's development to allow an opportunity for self-assessment. For example, you could simply ask the manager for an assessment of whether the goals and objectives were achieved successfully.

Finally, it's beneficial to suggest options for future improvement. You can even help the manager develop a plan to improve performance going forward. Or you could offer comments from observations you've made during the coaching process.

Techniques to assess performance

One of the challenges of managing experienced managers is tackling performance issues without undermining the manager's authority. When a manager isn't performing as expected, this affects the performance and motivation of the manager's entire team.

Poor performing managers often resist responsibility and blame failures on others. They tend to complain about their workload and colleagues. Such managers can stifle innovation and delay positive change in the organization. As a result, their actions can have a widespread effect on the organization.

There are some specific methods to help you assess experienced managers' performance:

- observe their availability and approachability
- manage by walking around and interviewing
- review their calendars and daily activities
- look out for telltale signs of bad management, and
- check whether the manager's focus is on the team rather than broader functions and the organization

Observe availability

Observing how available and approachable a manager is can tell you a lot about the manager's relationship with others. Is the manager available to direct reports to communicate company news? Can employees reach the manager easily in times of crisis?

A good manager will hold regular meetings and communicate relevant information without delay. A manager's approachability will tell you how others view the manager. For example, employees are often wary of a bad manager and will interact with the manager only when necessary.

Manage by walking around

You can assess your manager by seeking feedback from other employees. Do employees understand not just the tasks that need to be completed, but why these tasks are important? You can establish relationships with people in the manager's department by walking around the office and chatting to employees.

For example, you could ask questions such as, "What are your priorities today?" "When did you last speak to your manager?" or "Are you happy on the job?" Pay attention to what employees say and what they don't say. Silence can speak volumes.

Review activities

An ineffective manager will likely have poor time management skills. Often the manager will fail to delegate and get too involved in operational tasks. Reviewing a manager's calendar can tell you what the manager spends time on.

For example, is the manager focused on personal work, or on the team's collective work? Does the manager allocate sufficient time for developing the team through follow-ups, coaching, support, and training?

Look out for signs

There will inevitably be clues or telltale signs that the manager isn't managing well or performing as expected. For example, typical signs include high absenteeism within the team, frequent missed deadlines, and high staff turnover.

Furthermore, there'll probably be complaints from other departments or clients. Chances are that if you don't see these key signs, the manager is doing a fairly good job.

Check manager's focus

An effective manager will focus on the broader organizational goals rather than on the operational tasks of the team. The effective manager will instill a sense of belonging. An ineffective manager focuses too much on the wrong tasks – for example, taking over a team leader's role of managing administrators.

An ineffective manager may also focus too much on the department, rather than the broader organization. For example, say a manager collects some client information, but doesn't check if another internal department already has the information. This would be a waste of company resources. It would be cheaper and more effective for just one department to collect the information and share it with the other department.

Consider Grace, a senior manager in a banking organization. Grace decides to assess one of her managers, Amy. She begins by asking Amy a series of questions. For example, she asks Amy whether she makes herself available to the team. She also asks Amy if she's communicating company news regularly, and if her focus is on the organization's goals. Amy answers "yes" to all questions.

Grace then walks around Amy's department. She asks two of the banking administrators if they're happy working in the department and whether they have all the resources they need to complete their tasks. Both administrators politely answer "Yes." Grace then asks them if they've had any problems within the organization. They both answer "No." Grace is content and moves on.

In this example Grace's assessment of Amy's performance as a manager was incomplete. Although Grace directed relevant questions toward Amy and her administrators, she relied too much on firsthand information. It would be better to ask more open-ended and probing questions. Grace also should have also taken time to observe Amy. Furthermore, it would've been more effective for Grace to review hard

to delegate and get too involved in operational tasks. Reviewing a manager's calendar can tell you what the manager spends time on.

For example, is the manager focused on personal work, or on the team's collective work? Does the manager allocate sufficient time for developing the team through follow-ups, coaching, support, and training?

Look out for signs

There will inevitably be clues or telltale signs that the manager isn't managing well or performing as expected. For example, typical signs include high absenteeism within the team, frequent missed deadlines, and high staff turnover.

Furthermore, there'll probably be complaints from other departments or clients. Chances are that if you don't see these key signs, the manager is doing a fairly good job.

Check manager's focus

An effective manager will focus on the broader organizational goals rather than on the operational tasks of the team. The effective manager will instill a sense of belonging. An ineffective manager focuses too much on the wrong tasks – for example, taking over a team leader's role of managing administrators.

An ineffective manager may also focus too much on the department, rather than the broader organization. For example, say a manager collects some client information, but doesn't check if another internal department already has the information. This would be a waste of company resources. It would be cheaper and more effective for just one department to collect the information and share it with the other department.

evidence – for example, performance reviews and statistics on absenteeism and turnover in the department.

Now consider Carl, owner of a large business. He's decided to assess Holly's performance. Holly is the company's marketing manager, and she has a team of 12 people. Carl has reviewed the quarterly department statistics and is concerned that Holly's team is the only one with high absenteeism. Furthermore, three people have resigned from Holly's team in the last month.

Carl decides to review Holly's calendar. He notices that Holly is off-site a lot with clients or organizing events. She therefore doesn't spend much time in the office. On a day she is in the office, Carl observes that she's in her office all day with the door closed.

Carl then walks through the Marketing Department and asks some members of her team if they enjoy working for Holly. Two junior marketing executives admit that they don't have much contact with Holly.

In this example, Carl effectively assessed Holly's performance. Having reviewed some hard evidence, such as high absenteeism, he then observed Holly and interviewed members of her staff.

He concludes that although Holly isn't too involved in operational tasks, she's insufficiently available to her employees.

Managing nonperformers

After determining that a manager isn't performing well, you should follow certain principles to tackle the situation. First, deal with the problem immediately. It's also important to only hold the manager responsible for what's within that manager's authority. You should also make your expectations clear. It's also vital to keep a performance log to monitor progress. The final two principles are to work with the manager to search for solutions to problems and to follow up regularly to review results.

The first principle, which is to deal with the problem immediately, is crucial. Negative behaviors tend to become embedded in organizational culture, or become a subculture within it, creating a greater problem in the long run. Regardless of the spread of the impact, the morale of many employees will surely be affected.

Try to meet with the manager to discuss performance issues. Perhaps the manager needs more training or coaching. Are there external factors causing the problem? Make sure you understand what the problem is before you try to find a solution.

The second principle is to hold the manager responsible for performance issues. Responsibilities should match a manager's position within the organization. However, be sure you don't fault the manager for something beyond his control. The manager is only responsible for what the position in the organization entails, and those responsibilities should be clearly outlined in the performance objectives.

There are many ways to hold a manager responsible for performance issues. For example, you could involve a manager in the department budgeting process and assign responsibility accordingly.

It's important to let the manager manage. This is particularly important when monitoring the manager's performance. Continue to let the manager communicate with staff members and make decisions within the scope of the manager's authority.

The third principle to follow is to make your expectations clear. Managers must understand their responsibilities, the scope of their authority, the broader organizational goals, and their contribution to meeting those goals. For example, have current, accurate job descriptions, update managers' objectives as situations change, and make sure the objectives include required activities without gaps or conflicts. Also, make performance discussions a regular item during your one-on-one meetings.

Consider John, a senior partner in a law firm. He's assessing the performance of Ben, one of the company's managers. John has assessed

Ben's performance and concluded that it falls short of expectations. He must now take action to manage Ben's performance.

John requests an immediate meeting with Ben. He informs Ben that together they will update Ben's objectives to include specific activities to get his performance back on track.

In this example, John took appropriate actions to manage Ben's poor performance. Ben is now more focused on improving his performance. John will be available to monitor and support his progress.

The fourth principle is to keep a performance log. One way to monitor the progress of nonperformers is to document positive and negative performance. In the log, you give a detailed account of any issues that came up and explain how the manager dealt with each difficulty. Ensure the manager has a copy of the performance log, and agrees with your written observations and comments. This ensures that there is a clear basis for progress.

The fifth principle is to involve the manager to search for solutions to the performance problems. This will help the manager take responsibility for future performance, instead of feeling pressured into following orders.

Often employees are reluctant to discuss the real reason behind performance problems. For example, the problem may be a personality conflict with another employee, or perhaps an issue at home.

If emotional stress is affecting the manager's work, you can help by encouraging dialog, and actively listening to any concerns the manager may have. If the manager feels that you're working together, an intervention is much more likely to succeed.

Abu is having a regular one-on-one meeting with his direct report, Rick, a client services manager. Abu is concerned about Rick's performance because a high-profile client made several complaints about missed deadlines. Follow along as Abu discusses the issue with Rick.

Abu: Rick, I'd like to discuss your client Smooth Lane, Inc. I received a call from the managing director. It appears over the last two months, there have been six missed deadlines resulting in financial loss to Smooth Lane.

Abu is concerned.

Rick: Well, to be honest, Abu, I'm having difficulty with Smooth Lane's finance manager. He's so awkward and demanding; it's hard for the team to keep up with the requests.

Rick is annoyed.

Abu: Client management can be challenging. However, Smooth Lane hasn't made any requests outside the Service Level Agreement, so we have to honor any requests.

Abu is concerned.

Rick: But it's so frustrating! I'm starting to avoid talking to him altogether. I got a migraine last week after a meeting with him.

Rick is annoyed.

Abu: I didn't realize it was impacting you so much. We take employee well-being very seriously, so we need to find a solution that honors our agreement with Smooth Lane, but eases some stress on you. Any ideas?

Abu is concerned.

Rick: That's a relief. To be honest, I've been afraid to talk to you about it. I'll put together some thoughts and send you an e-mail by close of business today.

Rick is happy.

Abu: That's great, Rick. Then let's have a quick meeting tomorrow to review your ideas.

Abu is relieved.

Abu approached his conversation with Rick in the right way. It was evident that Rick was procrastinating, hoping that the problem would go away. As a result he was suffering from emotional stress. Abu used active listening skills to fully understand the problem and assure Rick that his well-

being was important. Finally, Abu asked Rick to suggest solutions to the conflict. Abu and Rick also agreed on an appropriate time frame for resolution.

The sixth important principle for dealing with nonperforming managers is to follow up. After the initial discussion to address the manager's poor performance, it's necessary to follow up frequently to review progress – at least every two weeks.

At every meeting, make sure that the manager's fully aware of the problem and its impact on other employees and the organization.

And finally, be sure to document each meeting.

Learning Aid - Action Planning Worksheet

To use this tool, you can print this document and complete the empty rows to keep note of your planning. Alternatively, you can use a spreadsheet or word-processing application to recreate the worksheet. You can then complete it onscreen and also save it as a template for future reference.

This worksheet provides an opportunity for both coach and coachee to record skill development needs. When completing this worksheet, it's critical to include specific measures of success and a target review date for any actions to be completed.

Action(s) to be taken	Measure(s) of success	Review date	Coach's role
EXAMPLE: Employee will refrain from interrupting colleagues during staff meetings	No interruptions observed during two successive meetings No complaints from other staff members	12/15	Coach will comment on progress after each meeting
EXAMPLE: Employee will take more time to explore clients' needs before matching potential products to those needs	Number of questions asked to identify needs Needs clarified prior to offering potential solution	After two more joint client meetings	Coach will explain the company's strategy of market-driven product development

Learning Aid - The Coaching Process

Step	Description
1. Determination and initial meeting	You must answer "yes" to several questions for coaching to be appropriate: • Does the person already have the skill or knowledge to perform this task? • Will the person be performing the task in the near future? • If you work with this person on a one-on-one basis, do you have the skills or knowledge to help the person enhance or improve the relevant performance area? • Do you and the potential coachee have the time to devote to coaching? If you can answer "Yes" to all of these questions, then you should schedule an initial meeting Begin with some positive observations and constructive feedback that focuses on the impact on others or the organization, and then agree on goals
2. Create an action plan	Include development targets and strategies to meet them Align targets to organizational goals Review objectives Take account of time available Account for any preliminary tasks such as training Consider others involved and who needs to be aware of the plan
3. Implement action plan	Organize some experience for the manager to practice the performance objectives Ideally, the manager practices the skills in a real-life environment where you can observe Arrange for the manager to shadow another manager or participate in a role-playing activity Progress should be recorded on the performance plan
4. Assess action plan	When assessing the action plan you should discuss the outcome of the actions, allow the manager the opportunity to self-assess, and give suggestions for further improvement

Learning Aid - Principles for Managing Nonperformers

Principle	Examples
Deal with problems immediately	Diagnose problem promptly with active listening skills
	Organize a meeting as soon as possible
	Ask probing questions
Hold manager responsible	Give responsibility in line with position
	The manager should be able to control the outcome
	Avoid blame
	Avoid undercutting authority
Make expectations clear	Have current, accurate job descriptions
	Update the manager's objectives as situations change
	Objectives should include required activities without gaps or conflicts
Performance log	Include a detailed account of issues
	Document positive and negative examples of performance
	Ensure manager has a copy
Search for solutions	Involve the manager
	Encourage dialogue
	Use active listening skills
	Agree on appropriate time frames
Follow up	Follow up at least every two weeks
	Make sure the manager is fully aware of the problem and its impact on other employees and the organization
	Document each meeting in the personal log
	If required, search for other solutions if performance still isn't improving

CHAPTER SEVEN
References and Glossary

A

active listening - The act of feeding back the literal meaning or the emotional content or both so the speaker knows the listener has heard and understood. To employ active listening one often has to paraphrase another person's worries and use acknowledgment responses.

authority - In terms of management, the right to direct a group of people or a situation and perform task delegation.

autonomy - The quality of having the ability or tendency to operate independently.

B

benchmarking - The act of comparing an entity's measurable performance against its performance from another time period, or the performance of another entity. For example, a manager could compare the data of a department's quarterly sales to the quarterly sales from a previous year.

brainstorming - The act of generating ideas, often performed in team settings.

C

coaching - The act of directing, instructing, or teaching a person or group of people to achieve a specific goal.

comfort zone - A psychological and behavioral state in which individuals exist and function in an anxiety-neutral condition.

corporate culture - The shared values and goals of an organization, which often lead to a general shared atmosphere.

cross-functional - Organizations or groups where different skills are used to achieve a common goal.

D

delegation - A management approach in which the leader assigns decision-making authority to others.

F
feedback - An evaluative response.
forcefield analysis - A problem-solving technique that aims to identify supporting and opposing factors relative to achieving a particular objective.
G
goals - Quantifiable aims used to measure progress toward an end result.
grooming an employee - The act of preparing an employee for a specific position or purpose.
H
high-maintenance employee - An employee who takes more effort to manage than other employees.
I
innovation - The act of introducing something new and improved to a product, service, or process.
intellectual capital - The collective knowledge of the individuals in an organization.
J
job sculpting - A technique that matches the interests and aptitudes of employees to the work they do.
L
leadership - A process of directing, influencing, or motivating others to achieve a common goal.
M
mentoring - A mutually beneficial relationship in which an experienced person, such as a manager, guides a coworker, sharing experiences and imparting knowledge and confidence.
micromanagement - A leadership style in which a manager or other leader closely monitors and/or exerts a large amount of control on the activities of a person or group, often to the detriment of the organization.
mission statement - A concise description of the aim of a project or organization.
morale - The general mood of a group of people.
motivation - Encouragement through incentive.
N
new job remorse - The uncertainty and doubt some new managers experience about their new positions.
O
organizational silo - An informal organizational structure that occurs when functional units work in isolation without considering the effect their actions have on the rest of the organization.
P

performance review - A mechanism for regular discussion and evaluation of an employee's job performance. Performance reviews are often one- on-one discussions between a manager and a subordinate, and cover quantifiable job responsibilities.

R

retention strategy - A plan that aims to keep workers, and prevent them from looking for other places of employment.

S

salary - Regular compensation paid to an employee as a condition of employment. Salary is generally computed on an annual or monthly basis.

SMART aims - An acronym for Smart, Measurable, Attainable, Realistic, and Timely, which describe the desirable features that goals and aims should possess.

stakeholder analysis - A technique that aims to determine and evaluate the priorities, requirements, and objectives of the key individuals likely to affect or be affected by a particular project.

sub-optimization - When an apparent benefit for a function in an organization harms the entire organization.

synergy - A state in which two or more things work together to produce an effect greater than the sum of their individual effects.

1. *How to Build A High-Performance Organization: A Global Study of Current Trends and Possibilities 2007-2017* - American Management Association, 2007
2. *Performance Management: Finding the Missing Pieces (To Close the Intelligence Gap)* - Gary Cokins, 2004
3. *Cross-Functional Cooperation The Project Management Institute Project Management Handbook* - Jeffrey K. Pinto, Jossey-Bass - 1998
4. *Cross-Functional Teams :Working with Allies, Enemies, and Other Strangers* - Glenn M. Parker, Jossey-Bas, 2003
5. *The Visible Ops Handbook: Starting ITIL in 4 Practical Steps* - Kevin Behr, Gene Kim, and George Spafford, IT Process Institute - 2004
6. *How to Hire a Champion: Insider Secrets to Find, Select, and Keep Great Employees* - David Snyder, Career Press - 2007
7. *Becoming the Evidence-Based Manager: Making The Science Of Management Work For You* - Gary P. Latham, Nicholas Brealey Publishing - 2009
8. *High-Maintenance Employees: Why Your Best People Will Also Be Your Most Difficult and What You Can Do about It* - Katherine Graham Leviss, Sourcebooks - 2005

9. *Creative New Employee Orientation Programs: Best Practices, Creative Ideas, and Activities for Energizing Your Orientation Program* - Doris Sims, McGraw-Hill - 2002
10. *Advancing Executive Coaching: Setting the Course for Successful Leadership Coaching* - G. Hernez-Broome and Boyce, L., Pfeiffer - 2010
11. *Coaching and Mentoring: How to Develop Top Talent and Achieve Stronger Performance* - Harvard BE, Harvard Business School Press - 2004

www.ingramcontent.com/pod-product-compliance
Lightning Source LLC
Chambersburg PA
CBHW020924180526
45163CB00007B/2875